PLANNING PROCESSES AND MUSLIM RESPONSES TO RURAL DEVELOPMENT IN INDIA

Planning Processes and Muslim Responses to Rural Development in India

Dr. MUMTAZ ALI KHAN
Director
Centre for Research and Development of Dalits
Bangalore—560032 (India)

Uppal Publishing House
NEW DELHI—110002

UPPAL PUBLISHING HOUSE
3, Ansari Road, Daryaganj, New Delhi-110002

First Edition 1993
ISBN 81-85565-25-2

Printed in India

Published by B.S. Uppal for Uppal Publishing House
3, Ansari Road, Daryaganj, New Delhi-110002
Printed at Sainion Printary, Delhi - *110* 032.

DEDICATED

TO

My Late Wife

Mrs. Noor Ayesha, M.A., B.Ed.

Hindi Ratna.

who inspired me to give up my Professorship to serve the poor

Preface

The study on 'Planning Processes and Muslim Responses in Rural Karnataka' was funded by the Indian Council of Social Sciences Research, New Delhi. The title of the project as sanctioned by the ICSSR was actually called 'Social Mobility Among Muslims of Rural Karnataka'. For reasons, the title is changed.

It is generally conceded that studies on Minorities, particularly Muslims, are extremely limited. It is in this context that the ICSSR had earlier sanctioned a pilot project 'Muslims in the Process of Rural Development'. The present study is a major attempt convering the whole State of Karnataka based on sampling techniques. The total financial assistance extended by ICSSR is to the extent of Rs. 40,000/-. But for this liberal and timely assistance the present study would not have been possible at all. The author is grateful to the Indian Council of Social Sciences Research for this help.

I am greateful to the Dy. Commissioners, Tahsildars, Pradhans of Mandal Panchayats, Village Accountants, Head Masters and teachers of village schools, mosque committees and above all to the respondents but for whose co-operation I would not have been able to collect the voluminous data for this study.

I am particularly thankful to my wife, Mrs. Noor Ayesha whose inspiration and guidance enabled me to complete the study, inspite of several hurdles.

Let me also remember with gratitude Dr. (Mrs) Leela Dube, Sociologist, and also Prof. Saral Chatterji, Director of Christian Institute for Study of Religion and Society who encouraged me to take up research studies on Muslims.

I owe my gratitude to my staff, particularly the field workers, who had to face many odds in assisting me in my field work. Mr. Nair, Stenographer of the University of Agricultural Sciences did a good job in typing the manuscript.

Dr. Mumtaz Ali Khan

Contents

List of Tables

CHAPTER I

Planning Processes and Muslim Responses in Rural Karnataka

Statement of the Problem

The Five Year Plans have programmes for the development of all sections of the society. But they have also special focus on the weaker sections who could not take advantage of developmental inputs for a long time. It has set the perspective of reducing inequalities in the distribution of income and ensuring minimum needs to the entire community.

This philosophy is further elaborated as follows: "The concept of development with social justice represents a change in the approach to development and sets forth a new strategy in which participation by all the people is both the means and an end to development itself."[1]

When the question of Muslim development is taken up, the Five Year Plan document has specific answer. While explaining

1. Karnataka Draft Five Year Plan, 1978-83, P. 114.

the basic approach and programmes, it is said that "the basic question, 'who is going to benefit from a programme or policy' should form the main frame work of the plan strategy in the State.

Social Justice

The ultimate goal of development being welfare of the masses, plan programmes have to be so formulated and implemented as to ensure that as far as possible a large section of the society should take advantage of the programmes. Could welfare be considered as an automatic out-come of accelerated growth and investment? Past experiences indicate that it can not be so. Even increased production does not guarantee per so that the welfare of the people, particularly the weaker sections, is ensured. Economic welfare of the weaker sections depends upon the growth and distribution of income, ownership of means of production and growth and composition of production.[1]

The State has implemented quite a few important programmes for the benefit of the weaker sections. Some of these progrmmes are : Land reforms, land grant, Small Farmers Development Agency and Marginal Farmers and Agricultural Labourers Differential Interest Rate Scheme, Bank finance to artisans, regional rural banks, welfare of women, children, Scheduled Castes, Scheduled Tribes and Minorities. There are also schemes like sites and houses for the poor, restructuring co-operative system, Employment Guarantee Scheme, etc.

These programmes, as said earlier, are applicable to all weaker sections which term includes minorities as seen in the Five Year Plan documents. Muslims as a numerically dominant minority group are also expected to reap the benefits.

The State Government has set up a few organisations to take care of the needs of the minorities. Of them, the Minority

1. Op. cit.

Commission, the Minority Development Corporation and the Directorate of Backward Classes and Minorities are quite significant.

The Minority Commission conducted two major conferences to discuss the socio-economic problems of the minorities. The recommendations of the commission are before the State Government. The Minority Development Corporation functioned for a brief period. It could not do much work for want of adequate funds.

Muslims of India have a vital role in the historical development of the country. Though they belong to an alien religion, Islam, they have adjusted to the local socio-economic situation, besides cultural environment. They have ruled at the Central level besides in many States for a long time. Even after the establishment of the British Raj, they continued to rule in some states like Bhopal, Hyderabad, Junagad and a few others.

With the advent of independence, the political scenerio started changing. While the Congress Government was established at the Centre, a few State like Hyderabad, Mysore, Bhopal, Travancore, etc. still continued to be under the kings. Muslims had their share. In course of time, kingship was removed and democratic governments were established.

After the establishment of democratic governments in all the States in India, power of the people began to play its role. Number became dominant along with the conventional caste system. Religion thus came to surface in a different form. Thus both religion and caste started having their impact on the political parties and voters. Muslims could no longer retain their supremacy in the power struggle excepting in a few areas where they are numerically dominant.

The share of the Muslims with a little more than 80 million population in the country in all development works was questioned. On the one hand, Muslims do feel that they are discriminated and deprived of developmental gains. Five Year Plans had no relevance to Muslim development. On the other, some groups among the Hindus have started attacking the Govenment for 'appearing the minorities'. There are hardly any research studies or any other method of providing reliable evidences to prove or disprove the question of Muslim development.

The Indian Council of Social Sciences Research, New Delhi, granted a pilot Project "Muslims in the Process of Rural Development". The ICSSR did not favour a major project for the simple reason that in the absence of any studies on Muslims it would be desirable to undertake a small, pilot study to gain experience and insights and then think of any major Project. Thus, the author completed the pilot project covering a few villages in Bangalore and Kolar districts of Karnataka State. The Project report was submitted to ICSSR.

Thereafter, the author submitted a major Project proposal originally designated as "Social Mobility and Responses of Muslims to Rural Development". The Project proposal was redesignated as "Planning Processes and Muslims Responses in Rural Karnataka" to suit the objectives of the project.

The two major areas for investigation, are economic development and Muslims participation, and educational development and Muslim participation.

The study aims at making a thorough examination of the awareness and participation. Since a sizeable population of the Muslims is involved in agricultural operation, it is desirable to analyse the various farming activities in which they are engaged. Muslims are also involved in a number of rural industries besides petty business. They have a tendency to take up such works which give them independent status. They are expected to take advantage of the various technologies and the change-agents. In other words, Muslims should be in a position to improve their economic status and contribute to the development in the rural areas.

Similarly, the State has introduced a number of educational programmes for both children and adults, men and women. Education is a pre-requisite for any type of development since the very values and attitudes are shaped by education. Education is, therefore, a very important instrument for social change in the Muslim Community too. Muslims are expected to take advantage of these facilities.

The pilot study conducted by the author earlier covered both economic and educational advancement of the Muslims. But the findings of the study highlight the poor response of Muslims in the two selected areas and the reasons for this. The two districts were selected earlier on the basis of convenience and therefore, can not give a representative character applicableto the whole State. Even the consultant of the ICSSR has expressed his view that broader and deeper studies are needed to understand the problem and more sympathetic and secular approach to the solution of it.

Literature

Research studies on Muslims are mostly confined to religious, political and cultural aspects, both at the State level and at the All India level. So far as economic and educational aspects are concerned, there are very few studies. In fact, the pilot study conducted by the author of this project proposal is perhaps one of the earliest attempts in this direction. However, there are some works completed by a few scholars which partly or fully touched the Muslim dimension. Mujeeb presents values in relation to education in his book "Education and traditional values". Madan presents some information on 'Muslim communities of South Asia'. Imtiaz Ahmed's article on "For a Sociology of India" mentions the dearth of research on Muslims. Wadhwa discusses some safe-guards for the Muslims in his book "Minorities Safeguards in India". Karandikar analyses the conditions of Muslims in his book "Islam in India's Transition to Modernity', Satish C. Mishra presents the conditions of Muslims in Gujarat in his book "Muslim Community in Gujarat". Asghar Ali Engineer raises a fundamental question of the role of Muslim leaders in developing Muslims in his article "What have the Muslim leaders done".

But these studies are by and large too general and have very little information on the economic and educational conditions of rural Muslims. However, there are a few studies touching some aspects of educational and economic conditions of Muslims. Imtiaz Ahmed has analysed economic conditions of Muslims in his article "Economic and Social Change". He has also probed into the problem of the Muslim educational backwardness in his book "The Problem of Muslim Educational Backwardness in Contemporary India : An inferential analysis". A.R. Kamat has done some work on Muslim education as seen from his works "Literacy and Education of Muslims" and "Progress of Education in Rural Maharashtra". Mumtaz Ali Khan has made some studies on the economic and educational conditions of Muslim in Karnataka, in his works on "Sociological aspects of child development: A Study of Rural Karnataka", Muslims in the Process of Rural Development in Karnataka", "Muslims in Slums in a Metropolitan City", "Muslim Children in an Industrial Society" and "Modernization Among Muslims".

CONCEPTUAL FRAME WORK

Since independence, India has witnessed a number of development projects starting with the Community Development Project. Subsequently we have had Rural Development Projects and later on Integrated Rural Development Projects. Various specific schemes like SFDA, DPAP, Anthyodaya, Integrated Child Development, Adult education, Compulsory and free education, etc. have been introduced in the rural society to bring about radical transformation in the conditions of the people. The Sixth Five Year Plan has laid special stress on the weaker sections and the minorities. In other words, conceptually, all these schemes are aimed at "Development with justice". It has been well recognized that in a multistructured society like India, the various heterogenous social groups, some with advantage of being the majority and some with the disadvantage of being the minorities, will have to be at least equitably balanced. It has also been recognized that if any social group is allowed to remain backward, the whole social system will be adversely affected.

The backwardness of a particular group like Muslims may be both due to prejudices of the majority and the majority controlled administrative machinery. It may also be due to the inherent deficiencies, cultural constraints of the minoriiy groups themselves. Progress of such groups would very much depend upon early identification of such barriers to change and remedial measures to motivate people to participate in and contribute to development.

It is in this context that the findings of the present major study would provide scientific material to the planners, administrators and voluntary organisations interested in rural development in general and Muslims in the context of rural development in particular.

Broad Objectives

The broad objectives of the present study centre round :

(1) Assessment of the progress and problems of Muslims in agriculture, animal husbandry and rural industries with the help of relevant sociological variables;

(2) Examination of the progress and problems of education with particular reference to aspirations, perceptions, motivations, and values of education among Muslims : and

(3) Assessment of the relative educational and economic conditions of Muslims in comparison with the non-Muslims in the selected areas for this particular purpose.

Major Questions

A few major questions that are raised in the study are :

(a) What are the present economic conditions of the Muslims with particular reference to agriculture, animal husbandry and rural industries ?

(b) What are the social and educational conditions of rural Muslims ?

(c) What is the socio-economic status of rural Muslim women today ?

(d) What is the nature and extent of social participation of Muslim men and women in socio-economic development programmes ?

(e) What are the values and attitudes of Muslims towards land, animal husbandry, rural industries, etc. ?

(f) What are the developmental inputs known to Muslims ? What are the sources of information ?

(g) What is the role of Muslim Voluntary Organizations in rural development ?

(h) What are the problems faced by Muslims in availing themselves of the rural development plans ?

(i) How far the village functionaries and organizations are helpful to Muslim development ?

(j) How do the Muslims stand in comparison with the non-Muslims ?

(k) If there are significant variations, what might be the reasons ?

(l) What special efforts are needed to allow Muslims take advantage of rural development programmes ?

Research Design

The research design was finalised after a few preliminary exercises. The Pilot study[1] conducted by the author in two districts of old Mysore area gave adequate insights into relevant research design. Since the present study aims at drawing certain broad conclusions applicable to the State of Karnataka, it was felt desirable to make the sample area as representative as possible. Secondly, the broad objectives of the study and the specific questions raised also warranted to include different categories of respondents. Since the study focusses on the conditions of Muslims, the sample population has to include adequate number of Muslims from the different regions. Thirdly, it was also felt desirable to include some women respondents to find out the conditions of Muslim women. Fourthly, since it was felt useful to have a comparative analysis of the Muslism with the Hindus, the sample had to include some Hindus also. A further elaboration is provided a little later.

Besides the sample area and population, the various research tools to be employed to get reliable and meaningful data were also finalised after some discussion.

Before finalising the research design, the author of this project took several measures. Two small-scale seminars were conducted. The benefit of experts in the various fields were obtained. About 100 knowledgeable Muslims were contacted and their views obtained. Available literature was reviewed. The author also took advantage of the two State level workshops arranged by the Minority Commission in Karnataka as already pointed out.

Regional Sample

Karnataka gets the seventh place in India so far as the

1. Khan, Mumtaz Ali; Muslims in the Process of Rural Development in India, Uppal Publishers, New Delhi, 1984.

population is concerned. The total population of Karnataka according to 1981 Census is to the extent of 37,134,714. The major religious groups are: Hindus, Muslims, Christians, Jains, Buddhists and Sikhs. Their population is indicated in table 1.1.

TABLE 1.1

Distribution of population of Karnataka by religious groups (1981)

Religious groups	*Population*	*% to total population*
Buddhists	42,251	0.11
Christians	7,73.500	2,08
Hindus	3,18,52,029	85.77
Jains	2,84,508	0.77
Muslims	41,63,691	11.21
Sikhs	6,401	0.02
Misc	13,334	0.04

Source : Census of India, 1981

Muslim population in Karnataka is not evenly distributed among all the districts. There are some districts which are thickly populated and some thinly. Table 1.2 shows the distribution pattern. It is observed from the table that there is heavy concentration in North Karnataka region. Further, it is seen that there is a higher percentage of Muslim population in urban areas than in rural areas in Karnataka State.

The position of the selected districts is that three districts of North Karnataka, namely Bidar, Bijapur and Gulbarga and

TABLE 1.2

Distribution of Muslim population in selected districts

Districts	*Urban population*	*Rural population*	*Total*	*% to total state population*
Karnataka	22,36,265	19,27, 526	41,63,791	11.21
Bangalore	4,94,427	80,177	5,74,604	11.61
Kolar	1,80,974	1,80,455	2,17,429	11.41
Hassan	41,157	35,148	76,305	5.62
Shimoga	80,118	93,908	1,74,026	10.50
Bidar	72,840	1,16,215	1,89,055	18.99
Gulbarga	1,61,537	1,98,484	3,60,021	17.30
Bijapur	1,37,217	1,72,132	3,09,349	12.88
Dharwar	2,51,769	2,14,848	4,66,617	15.84

Source : Census of India (Karnataka) 1981

only one district, namely Shimoga of old Mysore area have higher percentage of rural population. It means one sample district in North Karnataka and three districts of old Mysore area have higher percentage of urban population.

The sample districts are generally selected on the basis of rural population excepting in the case of Dharwar in North Karnataka region and Hassan district in old Mysore area. The difference between the rural population of Dharwar and North Kanara and also between Hassan and Chikmagalur is marginal. For the purpose of convenience, Dharwar and Hassan with a slightly lower percentage of rural population were finally selected.

Four districts were selected from the North Karnataka region and another four from the old Mysore region. From each district two villages were selected. Thus, in all 16 villages were included in the sample.

The selection of the districts was made with the help of Census of India 1981. Such districts which had a larger concentration of Muslim population were included. While doing so, internal regional and sub-regional variations were also kept in mind. Thus, Bidar and Gulbarga districts were selected from Hyderabad-Karnataka area and Bijapur and Dharwar were selected from the Bombay-Karnataka area. These areas represent North Karnataka region. From the old Mysore region, Bangalore and Kolar were selected from the Maidan area, and Chikmagalur and Shimoga were selected from the Malnad area.

When once the districts were selected, the next step was selection of the villages. Census records would give population based on religion only at the State, district and taluk levels. Village level population figures of Muslims and Hindus are not available. Even the Planning Department as well as the State Bureau of Statistics and Economics do not have the religion-based population figures at the village level. This led to practical problems for two reasons. The first related to identification of villages based on population of Muslims. The second was to identify Muslim dominant and Hindu dominant villages. This information was needed because it was pre-planned to find out whether there are any significant variations in the conditions of Muslims in these different situations.

This difficult situation warrant visits to district head quarters and meet people who had adequate and reliable knowledge of the Muslim population in the villages. In each district, a few villages were selected representing 100% Muslim dominant villages (MD), majority Muslim dominant villages (MMDV) and majority Hindu dominant villages (MHDV).

During the second round of visits to the areas, an attempt was made to scrutinise the reliability of the figures obtained. This was cross-checked with the village officials. Two problems of conflicts arose between what was given by the knowledgeable Muslims and the village officials. These are :

(1) Some differences in the figures given by the two sources in some cases, and

(2) The figures were totally irrelevant in some cases.

Since there was no practical solution to the problem, what was thought to be apt was to include only those villages in whose cases there was 100% or almost 100% agreement between the two sources.

The inclusion of the Muslim dominated and non-Muslim dominated villages was considered extremely relevant because of two reasons. First, no such studies have been undertaken so far. Secondly, the general expectation is that at least MDV should be more progressive than Muslims in NMDV. This hypothesis had to be tested. The districts and villages finally selected are indicated in table 1.3. The profile of the villages is also presented in brief.

TABLE 1.3

Selected districts and villages

Areas	*Muslim Dominant villages (MDV)*	*Non-Muslim Dominant villages (NMDV)*	*Remarks*
I Old Mysore area			
(a) Bangalore Dist.	Razack Palya	Harohally	100% MDV
(b) Kolar Dist.	Mohammed Pur	Kaiwara	
(c) Shimoga Dist.	Madaripalya Subebyle	Sasuvehally	100% MDV
(d) Hassan Dist.	Adampur	Gaurye Palya	
II North Karnatak area			
(a) Dharwar Dist.	Darga	Tadas	100% MDV
(b) Bijapur Dist.	Takiya	Darga	
(c) Gulbarga Dist.	Sethnur	Dandoti	
(d) Bidar Dist.	Hamehlapur	Gadagi	

BRIEF PROFILE OF THE SELECTED VILLAGES

Razack Palya

Razack Palya is a fairly big village in Bangalore rural district. It has a very interesting historical origin. One Razack Sab lived in this village. His was the first family there. He is dead and people consider him to be a saint.

There are 500 house-holds today and all are Muslims. No Hindu ever lived in this village, though the neighbouring village is a Hindu dominated village. People are interested in business. Sericulture is the major occupation along with agriculture. Barring a few houses which have RCC roofing, the remaining are all tiled houses.

The village has no bank. But the bank in Hosahally, neighbouring village, is used. There is a Government Urdu Primary School where both boys and girls study. There is big tank. But water is a problem. There are two borewells. There are no barbers, sweepers and washermen. There is one cycle shop. There is no Primary Health Centre. There is no private doctor also. There are no organizations of any type. There are 4 members of Mandal Panchayat.

Surprisingly, there are two arrack shops, though the population consists of only Muslims. There is a mosque. There is a no Baitulmaal (a sort of trusteeship institution encouraged in Islam for the benefit of the poor). Learning of Arabic by girls is encouraged.

The village is electrified. Streets are narrow and unclean. Drainage system is poor. Since the village is very close to Bangalore city, there are frequent interactions between the people of this village and their relatives, friends and business circles in the city.

Harohally

Harohally, a non-Muslim dominant village, is the village headquarter, located in Kanakapura taluk of Bangalore rural district. It is about 30 Km from Bangalore city. There are around 700 households. The name Harohally has some interesting phenomenon. It is learnt that the original inhabitants of this village were Brahmins and it was called Haruvara (Brahmins) hally (village). What was Haruvarahally is today called Harohally.

The major portion of the population consists of Bestas (fishermen) Muslims and Scheduled Castes. Bestas, Muslims and S. Castes account for about 210 households each. Brahmins and Lingayats (upper caste) have 20-25. While Brahmins and Lingayats are generally employed in Government service and some are agriculturists, Muslims are involved in agriculture, business and labuor. Scheduled castes are mostly farm labourers excepting a few families involved in Government service and agriculture. Bestas are no more involved in their traditional occupation. They are today involved in agriculture, manual labour and petty business.

The village has good roads, hospital, police station, co-operative society, hotels, primary and high schools, tap water supply, post office, bank and many shops.

Mohammedpur

This is a Muslim dominant village in Kolar district of old Mysore region. There are 120 houses of which Muslims account for 70 and the rest are Hindus. All these Hindus are Scheduled Castes and Scheduled Tribes.

The main occupation of the people is agriculture. Farm labour comes mostly from the Scheduled Castes. Muslim women are not involved in farm labour as they observe pardah. The majority of them are small or marginal farmers having mostly dry lands. Ragi happenns to be the major crop. There is a tank, but of not much use since water is a scarcity. There are two borewells for drinking purpose. There is a depot for the benefit of small farmers.

The village has a school. People are generally interested in sending their children to school, but upto IV standard. Thereafter they drop out. This is a single teacher school. There is also one Arabic School. Mostly female children attend this school.

There is no drainage. Roads are in poor condition. Sanitary conditions are very bad. There are buses reaching this village. There is a post office in the neighbouring village. However, postman comes daily. There is neither a local doctor nor any one comes. People go to the nearby town. There are no organizations of any type in this village.

Kaiwara

This is fairly big village in Kolar district. There are 450 households. The majority belong to Hinduism. Muslim households come to about 100.

The major occupation of the people is agriculture. Business is another important occupation. Muslims are involved in farming, both as a land owners and farm labourers. The major crop is ragi.

This is a village known for Hindu mythology. Pandavas were staying here for some time. There are three famous temples and one mosque. During the last 10—15 years the village had improved a lot as a tourist centre.

There is a blg tank. Drinking water in no problem. The village has Urdu and Kannada Primary schools and on High school. There is no hospital. People go to the nearby town as there are bus facilities. Roads are both broad in some places and narrow in other places. There are two rest houses. Drainage and sanitary conditions are good.

Madaripalya

This village is in Shimoga district of old Mysore region. This is very close to Shimoga town. There are about 500 house-holds and all but one belong to Muslims. Agriculture is the major occupation. While 100 households are involved in agriculure as cultivators, 400 households are farm labourers.

There is one Urdu School uyto VII standard. Nearly 50% children drop-out at lower primary level. After VII standard no one goes to high schools. There are no organizations like youth associations, Mahila mandals, society, farmers association, etc. There is one mosque. There are two dargas.

There are 5 bore wells drilled during the last 3 years. Roads are good. One road is asphalted. There are facilities for adult education. Electricity is available. There are no sanitary and toilet facilities. There is no washerman. But there is one barber's shop. The barber is a Hindu. Surprisingly, there is no mutton shop. People bring mutton from outside.

Nearly 100 families are involved in animal husbandry. Milk is supplied to hotels. There is no poultry and people are not aware of poultry scheme.

Subebyle

This village is located in Shimoga district. It has 450 households of whichMuslims ars 300 and Hindus are 150. The Hindu population consists of Kunchitiga Caste (17 HH) S.Castes (100 HH), Vaddas (40 HH) and Tamilians (25 HH).

Agriculture is the main occupation. Among Muslims only a few are cultivators and rest are farm labourers. Among the Hindus, Kunchitigas are leading farmers. Scheduled Castes are labourers. Vaddas and Tamilians are manual labourers.

There are Urdu, Kannada and Tamil schools upto IV Standard. Roads are not in good condition excepting one that is recently done. There is no hospital. There are no doctors. The village has buses. There are 4 bore wells.

Ahmadpur

Ahmadpur is small village in Hassan district. This is a backward village. It has 127 households. The majority of the population consists of Muslims. Though there are a few well educated Muslims of this village working in Bangalore, the village has not received enough attention for development.

This village has primary and middle schools. Children who pass out of middle school go to Arasikere town for High School education.

Drinking water is a problem. However, recently attempts were made to drill bore wells which work with the help of hand pump. There is a tank. Depending upon the rainfall, the tank becomes useful for cultivation of crops like rice, jowar, ragi and maize. The major occupation is agriculture. The majority have lands.

There is bus route to Arasikere. People go to Arasikere for many purposes.

Gaurapalya

This is a village in Hassan district of old Mysore region. It is a non-Muslim dominant village. There are 210 households of which Muslims account for 80 and Hindus for 130. The majority of the Hindus are Reddy-Lingayats.

The major occupation of the people of this village is agriculture, followed by farm labour and petty business. Among Muslims, the majority are farm labourers, followed by agriculturists and petty businessmen. There are 15 Muslims having land. But the majority have small acres only.

There are two primary schools (one Urdu and one Kannada) upto lower Primary standard only. There are one mosque, one Arabic school and one temple. There are no doctors. Village is electrified. Drainage system is good. One main road is good. Muslims live on the two sides of the main road and Hindus behind them. Houses are generally in good condition. There is a tank. Water is not a serious problem. Ragi and jowar are the main crops. Dairy is also encouraged here. But there is no poultry. There are no organizations here.

Sasuvehally

This village is in Shimoga district of old Mysore region. It is a non-Muslim dominant village. There are about 568 households, of whom Muslims account for 210 households and Hindus 358 households. The majority among the Hindus are Lingayats, followed by the Scheduled Castes.

While 250 Hindu families are cultivators and 108 are farm labourers, among the Muslims 100 have lands and the remaining 110 are farm labourers. Muslim women also work as farm labourers. Among the landed Muslims, 25 are involved in petty business also. The staple crops are ragi, jola and paddy. There is no water problem for irrigation.

There are 2 schools (one Urdu and one Kannada). About 60% children go to school. There are 10 graduates including 5 girls. This village has fairly good percentage of literates. Female education is also better.

Where there is no poultry, 50 households are involved in dairy. Milk is sold and a part is retained for domestic purpose. There are no cottage industries. But there are 3 welding shops and 3 rice mills. There is one public Health Centre. There is one private doctor. There is also one Arabic school. There is one mosque besides temples. There are no associations.

While the housing conditions are generally good, sanitary conditions are bad. Water is no problem because of Bhadra Channel.

Tadas

This is a non-Muslim dominant village in Dharwar district of North Karnataka region. It has about 1500 households of which Hindus are 1150 and Muslim 350. The Hindus consist of various caste groups like Scheduled castes (80 HH), Lambanis (50 HH), Marathas (300 HH), Lingayats (200 HH), Brahmins (100 HH) and others.

Agriculture is the major occupation. Paddy is grown if the tank has water. If no rains, people grow cotton, jowar and green gram. Business is another important occupation. Farm labour is the general occupation of all those who do not have land.

There are Kannada and Urdu Primary schools. There is also one High School. There is one Arabic Madrasa. There are three rice mills. There is one post office and police station. The village has a Government hospital. Animal husbandry is also there, but limited number of families are involved. Roads are good. There is electricity.

Darga

This is also in Darwar district. The population is 100% Muslims. There are 300 households. The villages has derived its name from a famous Muslim saint.

Agriculture is the major occupation, followed by farm labour. There are 200 households involved in agriculture. There are 40 big land owners who have about 10 acres each. The rest are all small farmers. Nearly 100 families are engaged in farm labour. Paddy is grown if there is rainfall. Otherwise, ragi and jawar are grown.

This village has no society, bank and hospital. People have to visit the neighbouring village for works connected with these institutions.

Some people have animals. They have one or two animals. There are a few bullocks for agriculture purpose. About 50 households have milching cows. There are no small scale industries.

Only 2 persons have private borewells for agriculture purposes. Government have not given anything. Both are hand bore pumps. Poultry is not found in this village. Sheep are owned by 25 households.

Sanitary facilities are extremely poor. Only a few houses have toilet facilities. Nearly 40% houses are electrified. Street lights are poorly maintained.

Takiya

This village is located in Bijapur district. There are in all 150 families. Muslims account for 100 families and Hindus for 50 families. Among the Hindus, Scheduled Castes account for the largest number. While among the the Muslims, 25 families are farmers, 10 farm labourers, the rest are involved in masonary and other works. Scheduled Castes are mostly masonary workers and munual labourers.

There is one Kannada school upto VII Standard. All Muslim children attend this Kannada school. Children generally attend the school. Because of its being close to Bijapur city, there has been a gradual change in the various types of technology. Water for irrigation is a big problem now. Due to paucity of water, people do not keep animals. There is no poultry. There are no small scale industries. There are no good roads. Village has electricity. Houses are poor and old.

Durga

This village is in Bijapur taluk and is a non-Muslim dominant village. There are 360 households of which Muslims account for 150 and Hindus 210. The Hindu population consists of 102 families of Scheduled Castes, 100 families of Lingayats and 60 families of Kurubas (Shepherds).

While the major occupation of the Lingayats is agriculture, the major occupation of Muslims and Scheduled Castes is farm labour. Lingayats have a larger portion of a land. Only 20

Muslims have land which is generally dry land. Excepting one Scheduled castes, the remaining Scheduled Castes are all farm labourers. Muslim as well as the Scheduled Caste women do all types of labour.

There is one Kannada school. There are no other institutions or organisations. Roads are in poor shape. The village has electricity. Water is a problem. Dairy is not found here.

Sethanur

This is a village located in Gulbarga district. Muslims account for a slightly higher percentage of the households. There are in all 230 households of which 100 belong to the Hindus and 130 Muslims. Among the Hindus, there are Scheduled castes with 50 households, Lingayats with 25 and Kurubas 25.

The majority of the population is involved in agricultural sector. Farm labourers account for the largest number. Water is a real problem in summer. Roads are in bad shape. There is no transport facility. Sanitary and drainage coditions are very poor. There is neither general hospital nor veterinary hospital. People have mostly dry land. Animal husbandry conditions are very poor.

There is only one Kannada school. There is no Urdu school. There are no organizations of any type.

Dandoti

This is a village with its own interesting historical background located in Gulbarga district. There are 900 households of which Muslims account for 400 and the remaining 500 belong to Hindus. Among the Hindus, a caste called Kooli has the largest number with 225 households. Lingayats come next with 150 households, and Scheduled castes with 100. The rest belong to different caste groups.

The major occupation of the people is agriculture. However, agricultural labour has the largest number of

Muslims as well as Hindus. Animal husbandry has engaged 60 families. Poultry and sheep are not found here. Water is a scarcity. There is no milk co-operative society now. There is a post office. There is only one old building in which Uurdu and Kannada medium schools are located. This is run on shift system. During the rainy season, water gets in from the ceiling. There is no Arabic school. There are 3 mosques.

Gadgi

This village is located in Bidar district. It is a non-Muslim dominant village. There are 425 households of which Hindus are 305, Muslims are 70 and Christians 50. This village is 15 miles from Bidar. Among the Hindus, Lingayats have the largest number of households with 100, followed by kurubas and Scheduled castes.

Agriculture is the major occupation, followed by dairy. About 90% land is dryland. Major crops are Jowar, groundnut and sunflower, Most of the people have buffaloes purchased out of their own money excepting in a few cases where the people got then from the Government. There is no well water for agriculture. Dairy has lot of scope because of the proximity to Bidar city. There is a great scope for vegetables for the same reason.

The roads are in bad shape. There is one borewell for drinking purpose and there is no problem. There are 5 temples and one mosque. There is one Upper Primary Kannada School.

There is no Urdu school. There is no drainage facility. There is street light and about 100 houses are electrified.

Hameelapur

This is a village which is located in Bidar district. It has 150 house holds of which Muslims are 100. It is very close to Bidar.

Agriculture is the main occupation. Nearly 90% people have lands, but small in size not exceeding 5 acres of dry land. The main crops are jowar and greengram. There are 20 open wells.

There is one Urdu Primary school upto IV standard. Almost every house has a cow or buffalo. Milk is supplied to Bidar. But there is no milk society. There is one mosque. Arabic Madrasa has been well established. There is no hospital. There are no private doctors. People have to go to Bidar. Most of the houses are electrified. There are street lights. There are 5 borewells for drinking purpose. The main road is good. Sanitary conditions are not bad compared to other villages.

Population

It was pre-determined to include a total sample of 800 of which 100 could be women and 200 non-Muslims for a comparative study. But the total sample was increased to 1042 of which 120 were Muslism women and 200 were Hindus. This change were found necessary during to field investigation.

The main respondents were 722 adult Muslims. The respondents were heads of the families in all cases barring in a few cases where the next eldest adults were contacted in the absence of the heads of families. Further, barring 18 cases of female adults, all the remaining were adult males.

The exact sample of the principal respondents was drawn after making certain exercises. To start with, in each selected village the total number of Muslims and Hindu households were gathered from the local officials. Then proportionate sample was drawn from each village keeping the total number of respondents in mind. This resulted in certain variations in the number of respondents from village to village. A minimum of 30 was ensured from each village.

Backward and Scheduled Castes

Even though the State policy is to ensure distributive justice to all sections of the society, it is generally felt that in practice the policy is not properly put into action. There are a number of forces which lead to inequal distribution of developmental gains. The major factor is the caste system. The upper castes have all the advantages as they are closer to power houses. The Backward and Scheduled castes are generally neglected. This has warranted special attention of the State.

Similarly, the minorities, particularly the Muslims, are expected to receive better attention of the State. The State is obliged constitutionally and otherwise to do some honest exercise to see that in the process of caste-based differential treatment, minorities do not become the victims of negligence and deprivation.

On the other hand, Muslims often allege that their conditions are worse than the Backward Castes and Scheduled Castes. Muslims get annoyed and frustrated because they had some significant say and share till independence. They were the rulers in many parts of the State besides the princely State of Mysore. They have developed a feeling that since partition of the country they are being gradually neglected. They also allege that the Backward Castes and Scheduled Castes who were working under them and who had a lower status have now atleast an edge over them.

There are hardly any studies made so far to prove or disprove this feeling. It was therefore, felt desirable to take some sample of the Hindu population to make a comparative analysis of the conditions of the rural Muslims and rural Hindus. While doing so, it was considered relevant to take the Backward Castes and Scheduled Castes. Inclusion of the higher castes was not necessary because their conditions are believed to be much better. The main reason is that they are the rulers today.

The term 'Backward Castes' includes a large number of traditionally neglected groups. Though a few such groups were seen in the sample area, only Kurubas (Shepherds), Kumbaras (Pottery makers), Edigas (toddy tappers) and Tigalas (hard working small farmers) were selected since they had sizeable population in the selected villages. For the purpose of this study, all these castes were clubbed and taken as one solid group.

The Scheduled Castes are the worst sufferers in the Society even today despite several measures for their development. There are special schemes for their development. There are quite a few major sub-groups among them. For the purpose of this study whatever types of Scheduled Castes were available in the villages under coverage were included. Thus in all, 200 respondents representing the Backward Castes and Scheduled Castes were included in the sample for a comparative analysis.

SELECTION OF MUSLIM WOMEN IN THE SAMPLE

Women in general are part of the weaker sections of the society. Muslim women are still worse. Though the Holy Prophet emancipated women from the controls of the exploiters and gave them certain status, over a period of time, their status has gone down. There has been a loud thinking that Muslim women are ruthlessly put down and they are almost like bonded labourers of their menfolk. They are denied right to education, freedom of movement and the association. They are not allowed to have any say in developmental activities.

There are not many research studies on the socio-economic status of rural Muslim women. In a recent book "Status of Rural Women in India", the authors[1] have made a comparative analysis of Muslim women with women belonging to

1. Khan, Mumtaz Ali and Noor Ayesha, 'Status of Rural Women in India, Uppal Publishers, New Delhi, 1982.

Hinduism and Christianity. It is found in this study that Muslims however do suffer from many handicaps.

However, it was felt desirable to include Muslim women also in the present study. Conditions of Muslim women are analysed in two places. Under the general conditions of Muslims, educational and economic conditions of Muslim women are also noted. But in a separate chapter, certain specific issues are received for analysis. For this purpose, a small sample of 120 Muslim women was considered enough. This sample was drawn from North Karnatak and old Mysore regions.

Since the sample drawn was extremely limited, it was not possible to take a systematic sample. All that was done was that 60 women from north Karnatak and 60 from old Mysore regions were selected at random. All these women were literates, having studied at least upto primary level.

Sources of Information

The data were collected both through primary source and secondary source. The primary source consisted of the heads of households, village youths, local leaders, religious leaders, selected women respondents, village officials and village teachers.

The secondary source of information is the available published records like Census of India, State Government literature, etc.

Tools for Collection of Data

Three tools were employed for collection of data. These are :

(1) Interview schedule,
(2) Group discussion, and
(3) Non-participant observation.

Of these, interview schedule happens to be the major instrument. The interview schedule covered the following issues.

(1) Personal characteristics of the respondents;

(2) Family particulars;

(3) Educational progress and problems

(4) Attitudes and values towards land, agriculture, animal husbandary, rural industries, etc.

(5) Awareness of Programmes under Five Year Plans for development;

(6) Status of women and their participation in developmental processes;

(7) Comparative status of Muslims and Hindus

(8) Behaviour of Government officials towards the respondents

The draft interview-schedule was pre-tested in four nearby villages on a small scale. This warranted some changes and additions. However, the previous experience of having conducted a pilot study was very much helpful in finalising the interview-schedule. Comments of some social scientists were also obtained. A small seminar was conducted to get better insights. Discussions were held with officers involved in rural development and suggestions were incorporated in the schedule.

Tabulation and Analysis

Originally it had been planned to feed the data on computer. But on the advice rendered by experts, it was decided to drop the idea of using computer. Manual tabulation was found adequate. At the end of each day, information collected was counter checked.

Since the purpose of the study is to gather information on the present socio-economic conditions of rural Muslims, and enable even ordinary men and women understand the out come of the study, it was adequate to resort to descriptive analysis and use only simple statistics.

Arrangement

The data after tabulation and analysis were organized into seven Chapters as follows :

Chapter I : Introduction

Chapter II : Economic status

Chapter III : Educational status

Chapter IV : Awareness

Chapter V : Muslim women in the context of rural development

Chapter VI : A comparative analysis of the status of Muslims

Chapter VII : Conclusions and recommendations

Limitations and Difficulties

The findings of the study are confined to only village situations. Towns are excluded. Secondly, though the coverage has both north-Karnatak and old Mysore regions, two important areas, namely South Canara and Coorg could not be taken up. South Canara was earlier a part of the erstwhile Madras Presidency and Coorg was an independent state.

The Research team had to encounter quite a few problems. Transport was a major problem. Some of the villages had no bus facilities at all. And some of the villages could not be reached easily even though buses were available. Secondly, lodging was also a problem. There were also female investigators in the team. Thirdly, respondents were reluctant to co-operate in the beginning partly because of apathy of the Government in their case and partly because of loss of faith in the research work. In a few big villages lot of effort had to be put in to mobilize the support of helpful educated persons and through them further steps had to be taken.

It was really a problem to convince the people. Some would ask the research team to swear and say that they would really help them to come up. Some put questions on political affiliation of the research members. What interest the team had in taking up the study was another question.

Information furnished had to be cross-checked wherever there were doubts. It was also a problem to interview women respondents. Female investigators had to be employed for this purpose. Male investigators could not generally interview female respondents. Similarly, female investigators, particularly Muslims, could not interview male respondents. Some married women were annoyed when male field workers approached them for information.

CHAPTER II

Economic Status

Status is an indication of the high or middle or low recognition that a person or a group of persons get from the society. Status reflects the forwardness or backwardness of individuals or groups. Status could be ascribed or achieved.

There are various means through which status could could be identified and measured. These are economic status, social status and educational status. Each category of status is further examined in relation to certain variables. Which type of status influences which other type is debatable. Whether social status leads to economic status or vice-versa. Similarly, whether educational status leads to economic status is also a much debated issue. Hall[1] has observed that economic conditions per se do not determine the improved position of any individual in the social system.

1. Richard H. Hall, Occupation and the Social Structure, New Jersey : Prentice Hall, Inc., 1969, p. 256.

It is in this context that an attempt to find out economic as well as educational status becomes relevant. In general, Muslims, particularly in rural areas, are considered to be poor. Their participation in economic development to be poor. Their participation in economic development is below the expected pattern. But there are no specific studies either confirming or rejecting this notion. The present reference to the economic status of Muslims assumes more importance.

There are both general and specific schemes for the development of Minorities in the country. Muslims as a dominant minority group are expected to take advantage of all the plan schemes. The 20 Point economic programmes as well as the 15 Point Programmes are of great significance to the Minorities. These are in addition to the general provisions under the various Five Year Plans.

In this Chapter, the economic status of the rural Muslims is examined with reference to :

1. Employment status
2. Occupation
3. Income
4. Borrowing
5. Land holdings
6. Child labour.

Employment Status

The basic yardstick to measure the economic conditions of any given social group is the employment status. Whether the people are fully employed, under-employed or gainfully employed will follow subsequent to the employment status. This issue is discussed in brief here.

Table 2.1 has relevant data on the employment status of the

TABLE 2.1

Employment Status of Respondents

Status	*Old Mysore Area*		*North Karnataka Area*		*Total*	
	N	*%*	*N*	*%*	*N*	*%*
1	2	3	4	5	6	7
Employed	390	93.7	290	94.8	680	94.2
Unemployed	26	6.3	16	5.2	42	5.8
Total	416	100.0	306	100.0	722	100.0

respondents and table 2.2 has that of the members of the families of the respondents. It is seen that unemployment is no problem at all among the respondents. Almost all the respondents. Almost all the respondents (94%) are employed in general. The position is similar in both the areas. However, the position is slightly different in the case of family While 73% in general are employed, 27% are unemployed. This sharp difference is due to the fact that 41% females are unemployed. The situation is almost similar in both the areas.

Occupational Pattern

Occupational pattern reflects the social status of a person. It is one thing to say that a person is occupied. But much light on the utility of a particular occupation comes to surface only when we know the quality of occupation. What type of work a person does shows whether he is in the right direction for better progress and prosperity or is just helplessly involved in work which is of no significance to his development.

The occupational status of Muslims in the study needs to be examined with reference to traditional Vs. modern occupation, vertical or horizontal occupational mobility and so on. This is examined in brief here. Occupations of the respondents and their families are looked into. Further, what is more important is the involvement of children in work. Child labour assumes greater importance and significance among backward classes which term includes Muslims too.

Respondents' Major Occupations

Table 2.3 indicates that the respondents are engaged in seven major occupations besides in miscellaneous occupations. Majority of them in general are engaged in the agriculture sector. In this sector there are more respondents in actual cultivation than in the farm labour sector, the position being

TABLE 2.2

Employment Status of Members

Status	Old Mysore Area					
	Males		Females		Total	
	N	%	N	%	N	%
1	3	4	5	6	7	8
Employed	631	88.1	360	54.5	991	72.0
Unemployed	85	11.9	300	45.5	385	28.0
Total	716	100.0	660	100.0	1376	100.0

North Karnataka Area						Total					
Males		*Females*		*Total*		*Males*		*Females*		*Total*	
N	%	N	%	N	%	N	%	N	%	N	%
9	10	11	12	13	14	15	16	17	18	19	20
370	82.2	277	65.9	647	74.4	1001	85.8	637	59.0	1638	73.0
80	17.8	143	34.1	223	25.6	165	14.2	443	41.0	608	27.0
450	100.0	420	100.0	870	100.0	1166	100.0	1080	100.0	2246	100.0

TABLE 2.3

Distribution of the Respondents by Major Occupation

Major Occupation	*Old Mysore Area*		*North Karnataka Area*		*Total*	
	N	%	*N*	%	*N*	%
Cultivation	122	31.3	69	23.8	191	28.1
Agricultural labour	80	20.5	81	28.0	161	23.7
Industry	10	2.5	8	2.7	18	2.6
Industrial Labour	32	8.3	16	5.5	48	7.1
Government Service	25	6.4	15	5.1	40	5.9
Business	80	20.5	75	25.9	155	22.8
Tailoring	35	9.0	20	6.9	55	8.1
Miscellaneous	6	1.5	6	2.1	12	1.7
Total	390	100.0	290	100.0	680	100.0

28% and 24%. There are 10% respondents in the industrial sector. And here there are more industrial labourers than industrialists. While 7% are industrial labourers, only 3% are industrialists.

The term 'industrialists' would just mean small scale cottage industries—agarbathi, beedi, coir mat making, etc. Similarly, labourers are also found in the same trades.

One of the criticisms of the Muslims against the State policy is that they are not adequately represented in State services. In the present study also this criticism gets reinforced. Only 6% Muslims have found jobs in Government service. And again these jobs are generally confined to peons, attendants, clerks and teachers. In the group discussions with educated and elderly persons, it was brought to light that education has lost its charm as the educated Muslim youths remain unemployed and they have to do business or manual labour. "By educating our boys, we have lost money and faith in Government".

Business

Twenty three per cent Muslims are involved in business which is mostly in the nature of petty business. Some of them do seasonal business with fruits. They purchase fruits from producers and sell. Some commission is generated in the process, shop keeping is another common feature among Muslims. Men and women of the same families share the business activities. While men go out for field work or purchases, women manage the shop. Generally shops are a part of the dwelling house.

Tailoring

Eight per cent respondents are tailors. They generally own sewing machines. Some times they take the machine for hire. They get good income from this profession. In fact, they would like to be tailors rather than agriculturists. But there is a limitation. Not many can afford to get orders from the people. Tailoring work is generally done outside the house by men, while women work at home.

The occupational pattern of the respondents in the two areas is practically identical with slight variations in the percentages. There are relatively more respondents in the industrial sector, tailoring and cultivation in old Mysore areas rather than North Karnatak areas. However, in North Karnatak areas there are more respondents in the farm labour sector and business.

Occupation of Family Members

Occupational pattern of family members is presented in table 2.4. A vast majority of the members are involved in agricultural labour (41%). While males account for 35%, females are to the extent of 51%. This situation is quite interesting. There is a general feeling that Muslim women should not work outside the family. This is further conditioned that they should not work on the farms of non-Muslims. But in actual practice this type of thinking is not relevant. Acute poverty forces women to come out and take up jobs anywhere, according to the Muslim respondents. Women also say that what their menfolk earn is quite inadequate to meet the requirements of the large family in the context of mounting prices.

However, to the extent possible Muslim women would like to avoid working on the farms of non-Muslims. Their preference is to work on the farms of their relatives and other known Muslim land owners. Where they have no choice but to earn and supplement family income, they would not mind working on anybody's farm. This reflects the cultural pattern set in Muslim society and a certain amount of contradiction. The elders would agree that this cannot be avoided.

There are more farm labourers in North Karnatak areas than in old Mysore area. While it is 43% in the former, it is 40% in old Mysore. Females in both the areas account for a

TABLE 2.4

Occupation of the Family Members

Occupation	Old Mysore Area					
	Males		Females		Total	
	N	%	N	%	N	%
1	2	3	4	5	6	7
Cultivation	120	19.0	20	5.6	140	14.1
Agricultural labour	200	31.7	195	54.2	395	39.9
Industry	40	6.4	15	4.2	55	5.6
Industrial labour	50	7.9	25	6.9	75	7.6
Government service	56	8.8	26	7.2	82	8.2
Business	100	15.9	30	8.3	130	13.1
Tailoring	60	9.5	40	11.1	100	10.1
Miscellaneous	05	0.8	09	2.5	14	1.4
Total	631	100.0	360	100.0	991	100.0

North Karnataka Area						Total					
Males		Females		Total		Males		Females		Total	
N	%	N	%	N	%	N	%	N	%	N	%
8	9	10	11	12	13	14	15	16	17	18	19
70	18.9	15	5.4	85	13.2	190	19.0	35	5.5	225	13.7
150	40.5	129	46.6	279	43.1	350	35.0	324	50.9	674	41.1
26	5.4	16	5.8	36	5.6	60	6.0	31	4.9	91	5.6
30	8.2	35	12.6	65	10.0	80	8.0	60	9.4	140	8.5
25	6.8	20	7.2	45	7.0	81	8.1	46	7.2	127	7.8
35	9.5	25	9.0	60	9.3	135	13.5	55	8.6	190	11.6
28	7.5	21	7.6	49	7.5	88	8.7	61	9.6	149	9.1
12	3.2	16	5.8	28	4.3	17	1.7	25	3.9	42	2.6
370	100.0	277	100.0	647	100.0	1001	100.0	637	100.0	1638	100.0

higher percentage than the males. However, the gap between the males and females is very much less in North Karnatak. While males account for 40.5%, females for 46.6%. But in Old Mysore area males are to the extent of 31.7%, while females 54.2%.

The second area of Muslims' involvement in agricultural sector is in actual farming as land owners. In general, nearly 14% Muslims are cultivators. Females are very much less with 5%. The position is identical in both the areas.

Thus, in the agricultural sector there are more Muslims involved in agricultural labour than in actual cultivation. The second feature is that there are more female labourers in agricultural labour sector than males.

Industry

The available data indicate that the participation of Muslims in rural industrial sector is very much marginal. The total involvement in general is just 6%. While women account for 5%, men have a slightly better percentage (6%). Area wise also the position is similar.

These are small scale industries mostly in the nature of beedi, agarbathi, mat making and broom making carried out at the family level. Further, these are all on small scale and not of much significance from the point of view of family income. Still respondents do recognise the utility since even this limited income provides them with some relief.

Industrial Labour

Besides being involved in small scale industries, some respondents are also working in industrial labour sector. The total number of such respondents accounts for 8.5%. A slightly higher percentage of women are in this sector.

Area wise the situation presents a contrast in between Old Mysore and North Karnatak areas. While 7.6% respondents are working as industrial labourers in Old Mysore area, 10% are found in North Karnatak areas. Further, while 7% females are in Old Mysore area, it is almost twice the percentage in North Karnatak areas. It is also found that while in the former area more men than women are involved, it is the reverse in the latter area.

The nature of industrial labour is tagged on to the nature of industries in which the Muslims are involved. There are no factories nearby. There is no assured labour too. These people work for wages in beedi, agarbathi, mat making, broom making etc.

Government Service

Government service is the only occupation that is always sought for. Muslims generally feel that they are very much let down by the State. The available data presented in the table indicates that 7.8% Muslims are in Government service which is far below their population requirement. Further, a vast majority of them are employed in lower grades. Though more males than females are in Government service, the difference is extremely marginal (1%).

What are the jobs in which Muslims are working ? It was ascertained that a vast majority of them are teachere in Government Urdu schools at the primary level. Some are peons, attendants, etc. A microscopic number is working in the class III cadre. However, even the peons are much better in terms of income, job security and other facilities.

Area wise the pattern is also similar in all respects, though in North Karnatak areas a slightly higher percentage of Muslim women are in Government service than men. However, this difference is not significant at all. It should also be noted here that these women work as ayas in schools as well as in primary schools.

Business

Muslims are generally known to be keen on business activities. But these activities are all confined to petty business. Nearly 12% Muslims are doing business. Majority of them have small shops attached to their houses. In other words, place of work and place of residence are generally one and the same. While 13.5% men are in business, 8.6% women also do business. This is really a matter of great significance. Muslim women doing business have their own sociological importance. It was observed that most of these women do business as petty shop-keepers. These shops are attached to their houses.

Women feel that their time is usefully utilised. When their menfolk go to the farms, women can take care of shops. They can attend to the housework too. Even children assist mothers in this type of business.

There are more Muslims doing business in Old Mysore area than in North Karnatak areas. While 13% Muslims are doing this in the former area, only 9% are found in the latter area. The second difference is that 16% men do business in Old Mysore areas, whereas women account for half of this only. On the other hand, in North Karnatak area, 9% men do business and the women also account for a similar percentage.

Tailoring

Tailoring is another pet occupation of Muslims. In general 9% Muslims are tailors. A slightly higher percentage of women are involved in tailoring than men. In the two areas under study, there are more Muslims ir tailoring in Old Mysore areas than in North Karnatak areas, percentages being 10 and 7.5. Further, while the involvement of men and women is equal in

North Karnatak areas, in Old Mysore areas more women than men are found, percentages being 11 and 9.5.

Another feature is that in the majority of the cases tailoring work is done in the house where these people reside. So far as women are concerned, it was observed that they do this work invariably in their houses.

Miscellaneous Works

A small number of men and women are involved in miscellaneous types of work. More women than men are involved here. Some such occupations are milching animals, domestic works, etc.

Respondents Income

Table 2.5 has data on the average monthly income of the respondents. About 62% of them have income not exceeding Rs. 300/- per month. Nearly half of them have no more than Rs. 200/- Another 20% have between Rs. 300/- and 500/-. The rest have income between Rs. 500/- and 800/- and a few beyond this too.

In regard to the two areas also, there does not seem to be any significant difference. However, while 58% in Old Mysore area have income not exceeding Rs. 300/- per month, it is 68% in North Karnatak areas. It would mean that the number of persons getting a small income of less than Rs. 300/- are more in North Karnatak than in Old Mysore areas. Similarly, there are more people in Old Mysore areas getting an income in the range of Rs. 300-500/- than in North Karnatak.

It was revealed in the group discussion that even this income, however limited it might be, is not an assured and easy one. There are occasions when the respondents have to struggle hard to maintain their families. Vagaries of nature do not assure regular rainfall and this would affect the prospects of both agriculture and animal husbandry. When crops fail, even the

TABLE 2.5

Distribution of Respondents by Average Monthly Income

Average Monthly Income in Rs.)	*Old Mysore Area*		*North Karnataka Area*		*Total*	
	N	%	*N*	%	*N*	%
Upto 100	25	5.7	30	9.8	55	7.3
100—200	80	18.0	85	28.0	165	22.0
200—300	122	34.1	92	30.1	214	32.5
300—400	46	10.3	30	9.8	76	10.1
400—500	55	12.3	20	6.5	75	10.0
500—600	20	4.5	12	3.9	32	4.2
600—700	14	3.1	8	2.6	22	3.0
700—800	24	5.3	11	3.5	35	4.6
800+	30	6.7	18	5.8	48	6.3
TOTAL	416	100.0	306	100.0	722	100.0

farm labourers also suffer. Thus, the economic position of the respondents is alarming.

Family Income

The average monthly income of the family is indicated in table 2.6. About 68% of the families get an average income not exceeding Rs. 300/- per month in general. A further break up within this group shows that the majority of them get less than Rs. 200 per month. Those who earn above Rs. 300/- constitute 32%.

There is a significant difference between the males and females. Among the males 56% earn less than Rs. 300/- whereas among females a vast majority of 85% are found in this group. Further, as high as 71% of them do not earn more than Rs. 200/-. Though it looks apparently that the income earned by the females is not encouraging, it should be admitted that even this limited income is a boon to the family. There is another difference between the males and females. While about 44% males do earn more than Rs. 400/-, none of the females earn more than Rs.400/-.

There is some difference between the Muslims of Old Mysore and North Karnatak areas. While in the former area, 65% are earning below Rs. 300/- in the latter area 62% are found in this income group. None of the females in both the areas earn more than Rs. 400/- per month. So far as the males are concerned, there is not much difference. However, a vast majority of the women in both the areas earn less than Rs. 300/-. A further break up would indicate that among the females in both the areas, about 72% earn below Rs. 200/- whereas among the females in these areas, the number earning less than Rs. 200 is much less. It accounts for 25% in the Old Mysore area and 35% in the North Karnatak area.

Thus, it is evident from the table that the income of the Muslims is quite unsatisfactory and this is particularly so in the

TABLE 2.6

Average Monthly Income of the Family

Income Range (in Rs.)	Old Mysore Area					
	Males		Females		Total	
	N	%	*N*	%	*N*	%
1	2	3	4	5	6	7
Upto 100	40	6.1	80	22.2	120	11.9
100—200	121	18.6	180	50.0	301	29.8
200—300	182	28.0	54	15.0	236	23.3
300—400	66	10.2	20	5.6	86	8.5
400—500	75	11.5	—	—	75	7.4
500—600	40	6.1	—	—	40	4.0
600—700	22	3.3	—	—	22	2.2
700—800	45	7.0	—	—	45	4.4
800+	60	9.2	26	7.2	86	8.5
Total	651	100.0	360	100.0	1011	100.0

North Karnataka Area						Total					
Males		Females		Total		Males		Females		Total	
N	%	N	%	N	%	N	%	N	%	N	%
8	9	10	11	12	13	14	15	16	17	18	19
40	10.8	65	23.5	105	16.3	80	7.8	145	22.8	225	13.6
90	24.3	130	47.0	220	34.0	211	20.7	310	48.7	521	31.4
104	28.1	34	12.2	138	21.4	286	28.0	88	13.8	374	22.6
40	10.8	28	10.1	68	10.5	106	10.4	48	7.5	154	9.3
25	6.8	—	—	25	3.9	100	9.8	—	—	100	6.0
15	4.0	—	—	15	2.3	55	5.4	—	—	55	3.3
10	2.7	—	—	10	1.5	32	3.1	—	—	32	1.9
16	4.3	—	—	16	2.4	61	6.0	—	—	61	3.7
30	8.2	20	7.2	50	7.7	90	8.8	46	7.2	136	8.2
370	100.0	277	100.0	647	100.0	1021	100.0	637	100.0	1658	100.0

case of the females. The condition is better in Old Mysore than in North Karnataka.

This issue was further discussed with some of the respondents and other knowledgeable Muslims in small groups. This was needed because on one hand the available data supports the fact that Muslims suffer from low income, and on the other the data indicates that unemployment in not a problem. There seems to be a prima facie contradiction. This warranted further problems. The result is that both are correct. Women in particular are not fully employed. While in Old Mysore 45% are not employed, in North Karnataka 34% are not employed. Among the males it is 12% and 18% respectively. But what really emerges is that the nature of occupation in which the Muslims are involved does not provide them adequate or even reasonably good income. They are forced to do whatever work is available and earn whatever is possible. This is the reason for a high degree of frustration among them. Acute poverty had made them desperate and they would not therefore, hesitate to attack anybody. They are critical of the Government as well as their own people. Muslim officers, elite and others, are criticised. Even the research team was in a very embarassing situation. "What do you do after getting information about our pitiable conditions? You are wasting your time and our time. Will the Government listen to you?" These were the remarks of some youths in particular.

Borrowing

One of the main characteristics of Muslim society is the easy way of resorting to loans. Even when income is reasonably good, Muslims have a tendency to raise loans, often for consumption purposes. This is the popular notion. Hence it was felt desirable to test this hypothesis in the present study. This issue is discussed with reference to the quantum of loans, purposes of loan and sources.

Table 2.7 deals with the quantum of loans. Nearly 50% of the respondents have taken loans not exceeding Rs. 1000/-. A little more than half of them have taken loans not exceeding Rs. 500/-. The number of persons who have taken heavy loans exceeding Rs. 4000/- do not go beyond 11%.

The pattern is more or less similar in both the areas. The main differences between these two areas are:

1. There are more persons in the Old Mysore area taking loans between Rs. 2000 and Rs. 3000/- than in the North Karnataka area (14% and 9% respectively).
2. While 12 persons have taken loans between Rs. 10,000 and 15,000/- in the Old Mysore (4%), it comes to 3% in the North Karnataka area. Such small differences are found in other ranges too; some times Old Mysore and some times North Karnataka having an edge.

What is important is the number of persons who have raised loans. In general 72% have raised loans. In the Old Mysore area, the number accounts for 70%, while it is 72% in the North Karnataka area. This difference is too insignificant. However, the general notion stands confirmed that Muslims resort to loans.

Purposes

The next question is why loans are raised? When nearly two-thirds of the respondents do raise loans, the effect of taking loans depends upon the purpose for which it is taken. If it is taken for constructive purposes, particularly for business or any other income generating purpose, taking loans could be justified. Otherwise, loans will ruin the families.

There are six specific purposes for which loans are raised as seen in table 2.8. The majority of the respondents in general have raised loans for non-constructive purposes like marriage, and family maintenance. About 27% have taken loans for

TABLE 2.7

Total Amount of Loan Taken

Loan Taken	*Old Mysore Areas*		*North Karnataka Area*		*Total*	
(in Rs.)	*N*	%	*N*	%	*N*	%
Upto 500	80	27.4	60	27.3	140	27.3
500—1000	62	21.2	50	22.8	112	21.9
1000—1500	40	13.7	36	16.4	76	14.8
1500—2000	20	6.8	18	8.1	38	7.4
2000—3000	40	13.7	21	9.5	61	12.0
3000—4000	18	6.2	10	4.5	28	5.5
4000—5000	6	2.1	8	3.6	14	2.7
5000—10000	14	4.8	11	5.0	25	4.9
10000—15000	12	4.1	6	2.8	18	3.5
Total	292	100.0	220	100.0	512	100.0

TABLE 2.8

Purpose of Borrowings

Purpose	*Old Mysore Area*		*North Karnataka Area*		*Total*	
	N	%	*N*	%	*N*	%
Marriage	40	13.3	60	27.3	100	19.5
Business	20	6.8	21	9.5	41	8.0
Family maintenance	120	41.1	90	41.0	210	41.1
Agricultural development	40	13.7	20	9.1	60	11.7
Animal Husbandry	30	10.3	10	4.5	40	7.8
House construction	30	10.3	15	6.8	45	8.8
Any other	12	4.1	4	1.8	16	3.1
Total	292	100.0	220	100.0	512	100.0

development purposes like business, agriculture and animal husbandry. Of these three, more persons have taken for agriculture. Nine per-cent respondents have taken for house construction purposes.

From this it is obvious that Muslims have a tendency to spend as much as possible on celebration of marriages (19.5%) and family maintenance (41%). There are various compelling reasons for this, as ascertained in the group discussions. Extravagance is a deeply rooted tradition among the Muslims. The question of a balanced budget is a foreign concept to them. Un-Islamic customs have wrecked the family stability. Marriage is a very simple affair in Islam. But today the dowry menace has ruined them. People feel very bad. They are sure that no sincere efforts have been made to bring in the Islamic spirit into action.

The situation in both the areas seems to agree with the general position. The vast majority in both the areas take loans for non-constructive purposes like marriage and family maintenance. Though 41% in both the areas take loans for family maintenance, there is a significant difference in regard to loan for marriages. While 14%take loan for marriages in Old Mysore area, 27% take in North Karnataka area. So far as constructive purposes are concerned, it is seen that Old Mysore is better than the North Karnataka area. For such purposes, it is 30% in Old Mysore whereas in North Karnataka it comes to 23%. Similarly, more persons have taken loans for house construction in the former area than in the latter area.

Sources of Borrowing

Sources of borrowing play a vital role in the economic development of the poor. If the sources are genuine and do not aim at exploitation, then the borrowers are safe. Otherwise debtors will be economically ruined and socially oppressed. Secondly, compared to the past, now there are various governmental and quasi-governmental financial institutions providing credit to the poor in particular. Banks play a very useful and dynamic role. Thirdly, there are social legislations which ensure safety of the debtors.

Keeping all this in mind, it would be interesting to find out the sources of borrowing open to the Muslims in the rural areas. There are five sources as indicated in table 2.9. Friends and relatives still constitute the major source with 38%. Whenever these people require small loans, whatever be the purposes, they obtain loans from them, generally without interest. This is done informally without any rigid terms and conditions. Repayment is also assured. In fact, the respondents say that repayment is more certain in such cases than in the case of banks. They seem to be more bound by ethical considerations rather than legal.

The next important source is the money lender. Nearly 22% of the debtors have taken loans from the money lenders. These money lenders have to be clearly distinguished from the merchants and landlords. The former are professionals. Their means of livelihood is often obtained from the interest they earn. Respondents say that when they suffer from acute financial problem, they would be forced to obtain loans from the money lenders, sometimes in their own village and some times from outside. They try to avoid going to these professionals as their rate of interest is quite high and the borrowers have to pledge gold or other valuables.

Landlords come third with 16%. The borrowers are either farm labourers or tenants or even those who have nothing to do with agriculture. Landlords provide small loan without enforcing rigid, formal conditions. This depends upon the relationship between the borrowers and the landlords. Another important feature is that the majority of the landlords are non-Muslims. The Hindu landlords do not make any distinction between the

TABLE 2.9

Sources of Borrowings

Sources	*Old Mysore Area*		*North Karnataka Area*		*Total*	
	N	*%*	*N*	*%*	*N*	*%*
Money Lender	65	22.3	46	21.0	111	21.7
Bank	35	12.0	20	9.1	55	10.7
Friends and relatives	116	39.7	80	36.3	196	38.3
Merchants	35	12.0	26	11.8	61	11.9
Land Lords	36	12.3	44	20.0	80	15.6
Any other	5	1.7	4	1.8	9	1.8
Total	292	100.0	220	100.0	512	100.0

Hindu borrowers and Muslim borrowers. The financial transaction is said to be smooth without any problems.

Merchants form another useful source with 12%. They lend money to the small shopkeepers who take goods from them. In this case the loan is in the form of goods sold and the money due from that. Muslim businessmen take goods whenever they need and repay before they take again. The whole amount need not have been repaid, yet things would be given in confidence. Sometimes even cash is taken.

The last category is the bank. Nearly 11% of Muslim respondents have taken loans from the banks often situated outside their village. These loans are taken generally for productive purposes or at least for that reason (in its name). But the people are not happy with the banks because of various rigid formalities and delays. Respondents say that when they have no other source available, then only do they think of the bank. It is also possible that the banks insist on timely repayment and resort to punitive action against the defaulters. Some respondents said "Our family name is spoiled because of the public insult done to us by the bank officials. We are treated as criminals and sinners, if there is some delay.

What emerged in the group meetings is that the people also take it lightheartedly. They get the feeling that if they could successfully dodge for some time, the Government could come to their rescue. Loans might be waived. Actually this feeling is on the increase.

The position in the two areas is also virtually identical with the general situation. However, so far as landlords are concerned, in North Karnataka areas there are more persons taking loans from the landlords than in Old Mysore areas, the percentages being 20 and 12 respectively. But for this, there is no difference between these two areas. Muslims do not have that much of access to governmental and banking institutions for loans.

Land Holdings

Ownership of land is a symbol of status and sign of economic stability. However, extent and quality of land would have a greater bearing on the family life of the owners. Table 2.10 has data on the land holding status of the Muslims. About 60% of the respondents have land in general. This seems to be quite an encouraging feature of the economic life of these people. But, quality and quantity of land owned provide the real situation. A vast majority of the land owners are dry land owners. Further, 73% of them own dry lands not exceeding 2.5 acres. It means they are mostly marginal farmers. Only 25% have dry land exceeding 5 acres.

Wet lands are owned by Muslims. The majority of them (47%) have lands upto one acre only. Seventy eight per cent have wet lands not exceeding 2.5 acres. While 12% have lands between 2.5 and 10 acres, none have beyond 10 acres.

Only a small number of them have garden lands, the percentage being around 3. Virtually all of them excepting 2 persons have garden lands not exceeding 2.5 acres. In fact, a vast majority of this group has land upto one acre only.

Those who have a combination of all the three categories of land also form a small number of 18 persons. While the majority of them do not have more than one acre, none have more than 5 acres.

When the Old Mysore and North Karnataka areas are examined separately, what emerges is that there is not much difference in the pattern. Both in terms of quality and quantity, the two areas are almost alike with some minor differences as in the case of garden lands, where the majority in Old Mysore have lands not exceeding one acre. Whereas in the North Karnataka area, it is only 56%. There are also 33% respondents who have garden lands between 1.0 and 2.5 acres. Other-

TABLE 210

Types and Acreage of Land

Quantity (Acres)	*Old Mysore Area*							
	Only Dry		*Only Wet*		*Only Garden*		*Combined*	
	N	%	*N*	%	*N*	%	*N*	%
1	2	3	4	5	6	7	8	9
Upto 1	70	33.3	20	51.3	55	83.3	5	50.0
1.0— 2.5	80	38.1	10	25.6	—	—	3	30.0
2.5 – 5.0	40	19.1	6	15.4	—	—	2	20.0
5.0—10.0	15	7.1	3	7.7	1	16.7	—	—
10.0—20.0	5	2.4	—	—	—	—	—	—
TOTAL	210	100.0	39	100.0	56	100.0	10	100.0

North Karnataka Area							
Only Dry		*Only Wet*		*Only Garden*		*Combined*	
N	%	*N*	%	*N*	%	*N*	%
10	11	12	13	14	15	16	17
50	34.5	10	40.0	5	55.6	3	37.5
60	41.4	10	40.0	3	33.3	2	25.0
30	20.7	2	8.0	—	—	3	37.5
5	3.4	3	12.0	1	11.1	—	—
—	—	—	—	—	—	—	—
145	100.0	25	100.0	9	100.0	8	100.0

Total							
Only Dry		*Only Wet*		*Only Garden*		*Combined*	
N	%	*N*	%	*N*	%	*N*	%
18	19	20	21	22	23	24	25
120	33.8	30	46.9	10	66.7	8	44.4
140	39.5	20	31.2	3	20.0	5	27.8
70	19.7	8	12.5	—	—	5	27.8
20	5.6	6	9.4	2	13.3	—	—
5	1.4	—	—	—	—	—	—
355	100.0	64	100.0	15	100.0	18	100.0

wise as said earlier, there is not much difference between the two areas.

What is most relevant here is the fact that a majority of the Muslims suffer (low quality as well as small quantity of lands), as a result of small plots of land which are not always easy to cultivate. These are not economically viable. As small and marginal farmers, they have no option but to take maximum advantage of this inevitable land holding position.

What is more interesting is that, according to a large number of Muslims, the land ownership pattern has changed very much during the last two decades and this changing trend is moving faster during the last five years. Many Muslims who have lands have inherited from their fathers/grand fathers (70%). Only 30% have purchased lands. There was absolutely no evidence of getting land from the Government. Muslims are aware of the fact that the Scheduled Castes and Scheduled Tribes are the beneficiaries of the land grant policy of the state.

Some people remarked 'What Sir, who cares for us ? We are the most neglected section. Not only we are not getting any land grant patronage from the Government, but also we are losing our own lands and at the present rate, in another decade, there will be hardly any Muslim either having land or interested in land'.

These remarks made in group situation warranted further probe to ascertain the factors responsible for this changing scene. It was gathered that a vast majority of them have no interest in land ownership because land, particularly dry land, without necessary inputs is of no use. Some one said "It is only ornamental. We call ourselves landlord". Muslims said that getting loan from the banks is generally a great problem. They have the feeling that they are descriminated. Extention workers are generally more interested in serving the cause of the Scheduled caste/Scheduled Tribe because of special responsibility that the State has owned. Muslims also made it clear that they are not against such special provisions in favour of Scheduled Caste/Scheduled Tribe people.

There are some Muslims who have big wells. But water is not available in required quantity. They suffer a lot during summer. If some small help is rendered in drilling bore within the well, there could be some more water.

The second reason why they are losing interest in land is that rural social scene today is not conducive to Muslims, according to the leaders. There is no social security. Communal clashes in the towns and cities spread soon to nearby villages and Muslims become the victims. So, they dispose of their lands and migrate to places where they can expect better security.

Child Labour

Child Labour in our society is very common despite constitutional and legal prohibitions. No special group is perhaps an exception to this among the poor. It is generally felt that child labour is the major problem in the Muslim society, both urban and rural areas. In the present study an attempt was made to examine the prevalence of child labour in rural Karnataka.

Table 2.11 has statistical information on this issue. It is observed that there are 814 children employed as labourers. Out of them, 59% are in Old Mysore Area and 42% in North Karnataka Area.

In terms of sex, it is seen that there are more male child labourers in Old Mysore area than in North Karnataka area, the percentages being 59 and 41 respectively. However, so far female child labour is concerned, there are more in North Karnataka area (53%) than in Old Mysore area (47%).

TABLE 2.11

Prevalence of Child Labour

Area	*Males*		*Females*		*Total*	
	N	*%*	*N*	*%*	*N*	*%*
Old Mysore Area	346	59.0	108	47.4	454	55.8
North Karnataka Area	240	41.0	120	52.6	360	44.2
Total	586	100.0	228	100.0	814	100.0

Types

Employment is generally of two types, self-employment and employment for wages. While self-employment means involvement in one's own occupation or family occupation, employment for wages would invariably mean working under others outside the family circle for wages. In what form the Muslim children are employed is discussed with the help of table 2.12.

In general, more children are employed for wages, the percentage being 56%. Those who are self-employed account for 44%. The position is different in regard to sex. While 61% males are employed for wages, 39% are self-employed. In the case of female children, the position is reverse. While 57% female children are self-employed, 43% are employed for wages.

This variation between the male and female child labour was further explained by the respondents in group discussion. Parents feel that girls should take up work at home, whether for wages or otherwise. Sending girls outside for work is not generally appreciated. If only poverty forces, they send their girls outside the family circle for jobs. It was further learnt that even when the girls go out for jobs, they are generally employed by their relatives and known people. Parents avoid strangers. Another significant feature is that parents generally do not like to allow their girls to work under non-Muslims Some parents remarked, "If our girls are employed under the non-Muslims, it is a clear evidence of their total helplessness".

The position in the two areas slightly differs so far as female children are concerned. In Old Mysore area 69% girls are self-employed and 31% are employed for wages. But in North Karnataka area, 54% girls are employed for wages and 46% self-employed. This accounts for greater pressure on girls to earn to supplement family income.

TABLE 2.12

Type of Child Labour

Types	Old Mysore Area					
	Males		Females		Total	
	N	%	*N*	%	*N*	%
1	2	3	4	5	6	7
Self-employed	140	40.5	75	69.4	215	47.4
Employed for wages	206	59.5	33	30,6	239	52.6
Total	346	100.0	108	100.0	454	100.0

North Karnataka Area						Total					
Males		Females		Total		Males		Females		Total	
N	%	N	%	N	%	N	%	N	%	N	%
8	9	10	11	12	13	14	15	16	17	18	19
90	37.5	55	45.8	145	40.3	230	39 3	130	57.0	360	44.2
150	62.5	65	54.2	215	59.7	356	60.7	98	43.0	454	55.8
140	100.0	120	100.0	360	100.0	586	100.0	228	100.0	814	100.0

Child Labour and Age

The age at which a child is involved in labour, particularly for wages, has tremendous impact on the development of the child. Exposure to outside work involving difficult and time consuming nature of work affects the physical and mental growth of the child. In the present study, as seen from table 2.13, 19% children in general are involved between the age group of 7—10. Thirty five per cent are found in the age group of 11—14 and 46% in the age group of 15—18. In relation to sex, the position is similar excepting that there are more girls in the age group of 11—14 than the boys. In the age group of 15—18, there are more boys than girls, the percentage being 50 and 34 respectively.

Area-wise analysis shows that in the Old Mysore Area, a little more than 50% of the male children are involved in the age group of 15—18. Another significant feature here is that there are more female children (26%) than male children (19%) in the age group of 7—10. Further, there are again more female children in the age group of 11—14 years than in the age group of 15—18. In terms of percentages this comes to 39 and 31 respectively. Female children are more than male children in the age group of 15—18.

So far as North Karnataka area is concerned, the total number of child labourers comes to 42% in the age group of 11-14 as well in the age group of 15-18 years. Sex-wise speaking, there are more male children (46%) than female children (33%) in the age group of 15-18, whereas in the age group of 11-14 years, 50% female children as against 37% male children are found. In fact, it is in this age group of 11-14 years that we find more male as well as female children in North Karnataka area than in Old Mysore area.

One major conclusion that can be drawn from the above analysis is that in the general a little more than 50% children

TABLE 2.13

Child Labour in Relation to Age

Age	*Old Mysore Area*					
	Male		*Female*		*Total*	
	N	%	*N*	%	*N*	%
1	2	3	4	5	6	7
7–10	66	19.1	28	25.9	94	20.7
11—14	94	27.2	42	38.9	136	29.9
15—18	186	53.7	38	35.2	224	49.4
Total	346	100.0	108	100.0	454	100.0

North Karnataka Area						Total					
Male		Female		Total		Male		Female		Total	
N	%	N	%	N	%	N	%	N	%	N	%
8	9	10	11	12	13	14	15	16	17	18	19
40	16.7	20	16.7	60	16.6	106	18.1	48	21.1	154	18.9
90	37.5	60	50.0	150	41.7	184	31.4	102	44.7	286	35.1
110	45.8	40	33.3	150	41.7	296	50.5	78	34.2	374	46.0
240	100.0	120	100.0	360	100.0	586	100.0	228	100.0	814	100.0

are employed as child labourers which means that the provisions of Compulsory Education Act of 1961 are not complied with. This is more so in the case of girls in whose case 66% are out of schools.

Child Labour and Literacy

Child labour in relation to literacy status is examined with reference to the data presented in table 2.14. It is seen that in general 30% of the children involved in labour are literates. The rest of them are illiterates. Among the male child labourers 33% are literates and 67% are illiterates. So far female child labourers are concerned as high as 79% are illiterates.

The position is more or less similar in both the areas. In the North Karnataka area 83% female child labourers are illiterates, whereas among the male labourers 62% are illiterates, where it is 74% and 69% respectively.

It is thus evident that a vast majority of the child labourers are illiterates. But what is equally significant is nearly 30% of them are literates. Further, there are more illiterate female child labourers than the males.

Child Labour and Occupation

The various types of occupation in which children are engaged are indicated in table 2.15. In general, a vast majority of the children accounting for 78% of the child labourers are involved in agricultural and animal husbandry activities. A further break up indicates that 38% are involved in agricultural sector. Even here more children are involved in farm labour. So far as non-agricultural sector is concerned, children are employed in building construction (2.7%), Beedi (2.4%), Agarbathi (3.0%), Weaving (8.9) and 5.1% in miscellaneous activities.

With reference to the sex breakup it is seen that among the male children nearly 86% are involved in agricultural sector,

TABLE 2.14

Child Labour in Relation to Literacy Status

Literacy Status	*Old Mysore Area*					
	Males		*Female*		*Total*	
	N	%	*N*	%	*N*	%
1	2	3	4	5	6	7
Literates	106	30.6	28	25.9	134	29.5
Illiterates	240	69.4	80	74.1	320	70.5
Total	346	100.0	108	100.0	454	100.0

North Karnataka Area						Total					
Male		Female		Total		Male		Female		Total	
N	%	N	%	N	%	N	%	N	%	N	%
8	9	10	11	12	13	14	15	16	17	18	19
90	37.5	20	16.5	110	30.6	196	33.4	48	21.1	244	29.9
150	62.5	100	83.5	250	69.4	390	66.6	180	78.9	570	70.1
240	100.0	120	100.0	360	100.0	586	100.0	228	100.0	814	100.0

TABLE 2.15

Child Labour in Relation to Occupation

Occupation	*Old Mysore Area*					
	Males		*Females*		*Total*	
	N	%	*N*	%	*N*	%
1	2	3	4	5	6	7
Farm labour	98	28.3	13	12.0	111	24.4
Cultivation	42	12.1	—	—	42	9.2
Mending animals at home	80	23.2	25	23.1	105	23.1
Sericulture	50	14.5	15	13.9	65	14.3
Grazing animals outside	41	11.8	—	—	41	9.0
Building construction	10	2.9	—	—	10	2.2
Beedi	—	—	20	18.5	20	4.4
Agarbathi	—	—	25	23.1	25	5.1
Weaving	15	4.3	10	9.4	25	5.1
Miscellaneous	10	2.9	—	—	10	2.2
Total	346	100.0	108	100.0	454	100.0

North Karnataka Area						Total					
Males		Females		Total		Males		Femaels		Total	
N	%	N	%	N	%	N	%	N	%	N	%
8	9	10	11	12	13	14	15	16	17	18	19
80	32.0	35	29.2	105	29.2	178	29.9	48	21.0	226	27.4
30	12.0	15	12.5	45	12.5	72	12.1	15	6.6	87	10.6
32	12.8	13	10.8	45	12.5	112	18.8	38	16.7	150	18.2
—	—	—	—	—	—	50	8.4	15	6.6	65	7.9
58	23.2	15	12.5	73	20.3	99	16.6	15	6.6	114	13.8
12	4.8	—	—	12	3.3	22	3.7	—	—	22	2.7
—	—	—	—	—	—	—	—	20	8.8	20	2.4
—	—	—	—	—	—	—	—	25	10.9	25	3.0
26	10.4	22	18.3	48	13.3	41	6.8	32	14.0	73	8.9
12	4.8	20	16.7	32	8.9	22	3.7	20	8.8	42	5.1
250	100.0	120	100.0	360	100.0	596	100.0	228	100.0	824	100.0

which term includes animal husbandry also. Forty two per cent of these male children are involved in farm labour and cultivation. About 8% are involved in Sericulture. Thirty five per cent male children are involved in animal husbandry. So far as non-agricultural sector is concerned, it is seen that none of the boys are involved in Beedi and agarbathi works. While 3.7% boys are involved in building construction activities, 6.8% are involved in weaving industry.

So far as female children are concerned, it is seen that 57.6% are involved in agricultural sector. Here 37.6% are involved in farm labour and cultivation. In cultivation only 6.6% girls are found, whereas 21% work as farm labourers. 23.3% girls are involved in mending animals at home and grazing them outside the house. The other activities of the girls are: Beedi industry (8.8%), Agarbathi (10.9%), Weaving (14%) and miscellaneous (8.8%).

In relation to the two different areas, there is some significant difference in general. While the majority of the children in both the areas are involved in agricultural sector, 23% children are involved in mending animals at home in Old Mysore area. It comes to 12.5% in North Karnataka Area. Secondly, while 14.3% children are involved in sericulture in old Mysore area, there is none from North Karnataka area. Further, while 9% children in old Mysore area are involved in grazing animals outside the home, the number is large with 20% in North Karnataka area. Another important difference is that while some children are involved in Beedi and Agarbathi works in Old Mysore area none of the children from North Karnataka are involved here. Further, the number of children involved in weaving work is more in North Karnataka area (13.3%) than in Old Mysore area (5.1%).

In relation to sex, there is quite a lot of difference, both intra and inter area. In Old Mysore area, 28.3% male children are involved in agricultural labour, whereas only 12% girls are found here. In North Karnataka area not only there is a higher percentage of male and female children in agricultural labour sector, but also the difference between females of these two areas is quite significant. While just 12% female children are working as farm labourers in Old Mysore area, the percentage of female children in North Karnataka area is more than double (29.2%). While there is no girl working in cultivation of land in Old Mysore area, 12.5% girls are working in North Karnataka area.

Boys and girls are more or less equally involved in mending animals in both the areas with the difference that there are more children in Old Mysore area than in North Karnataka area, almost twice the number. Boys and girls are involved in sericulture in almost equal number in Old Mysore area, whereas there is none in North Karnataka area. There are more boys in North Karnataka area than old Mysore area in grazing animals outside the house (23% and 11.8% respectively). While none of the girls involved in this activity in Old Mysore area, 12.5% girls are involved in North Karnataka area.

Beedi and agarbathi activities are confined only to girls of Old Mysore area. Neither boys of both the areas nor girls of North Karnataka area are involved here. There are more boys and girls involved in weaving in North Karnataka area than in Old Mysore area. Further, girls account for a higher percentage than boys in North Karnataka area (18.3% and 9.4%).

Opinion About Child Labour

From the earlier analysis it is obvious that both male and female children are involved in economic activities. The reasons ascertained are :

(1) Poverty forces parents to allow children to earn as much as possible,

(2) children refuse to go to schools.

(3) they create problems at home if remained without any work, and

(4) children who do not go to schools learn atleast some work which will help them later on.

But are the parents really happy to allow their children take up jobs ? The question was put to the respondents. Their responses are presented in table 2.16. As hight as 64% respondents do feel that child labour is bad. While 17% say it is good, 19% remain neutral. Those who say it is good justify on the ground that children will be spoiled otherwise. They earn something. Further, a higher percentage of respondents say 'good' in favour of boys (24%) than in favour of girls (10%). Those who say 'bad' feel that child labour is bad for both boys and girls, more or less in equal number.

When analysed in relation to the two different areas, there is not much difference. A vast majority in both the areas say it is bad for both boys and girls. A marginally higher percentage of respondents say it is 'good' in North Karnataka area when compared to Old Mysore area, percentages being 18.7 and 15.8 respectively. Surprisingly, those who favour for girls account for 12.5% in North Karnataka area, while it is 8.3% in Old Mysore area. Further, among those who favour child labour in both the areas, a higher percentage favour for boys than for girls in both the areas.

Child Labour : A Case Study

Aslam Pasha is around 12 years in a Muslim village called Razack Palya. His father is a priest in the local mosque. Aslam studied upto III Standard. He failed in the examination. He was least bothered about the result. His father was disappointed and was very angry with the son. When he scolded and threatened him, the boy got disgusted and ran away from the family. After 15 days the boy was found working in a distant village, almost like a bonded labourer.

TABLE 2.16

Opinion of Children About Child Labour

Occupation	*Old Mysore Area*					
	Boys		*Girls*		*Total*	
	N	*%*	*N*	*%*	*N*	*%*
1	2	3	4	5	6	7
Good	14	23.3	5	8.3	19	15.8
Bad	36	60.0	40	66.7	76	63.3
Neutral	10	16.7	15	25.0	25	20.9
Total	60	100.0	60	100.0	120	100.0

North Karnataka Area						Total					
Boys		Girls		Total		Boys		Girl		Total	
N	%	N	%	N	%	N	%	N	%	N	%
8	9	10	11	12	13	14	15	16	17	18	19
10	25.0	5	12.5	25	18.7	24	24.0	10	10.0	34	17.0
25	62.5	27	67.5	52	65.0	61	61.0	67	67.0	128	64.0
5	12.5	8	20.0	13	16.3	15	15.0	23	23.0	38	19.0
40	100.0	40	100.0	90	100.0	100	100.0	100	100.0	200	100.0

When the father got this information, he went to that village with his wife. She succeeded in bringing the boy back to the house. The boy put one condition. "I will not go to school. Please do not force me. If you force, me, I will run away again". The mother promised him. Though the boy was then just 8 years old, he was quite firm.

The family is very poor with six children, mostly girls. The parents had no option but to allow the boy get some employment. The boy was given a job by a silk reeling merchant. He was started on Rs. 5 per day and this was increased later on to Rs. 10/- But he would get job for only 15 days on an average. He would give the whole amount to the father. When asked as to how he would spend the rest of the period when not employed, he said "I enjoy playing with my friends. I nicely roam about in the village"· "Do you feel bad for leaving the school ? His answer was 'Yes, definitely. I see some of my friends planning to go to high school. I learn that they become masters (teachers) and earn good amount. I now feel sorry for leaving the school. I wish I had continued". "Whose fault was it that you left the school ?" The boy said 'It is not mine. My bad friends misguided me. They showed me their income. They were happy. In my home there was nothing but poverty. I would not get my food in time. I used to go to school late. The teacher used to beat me. I left the school. Of course, partly I am also wrong".

"Are you prepared to go to school now? He said, 'how can it be, not possible. I can not sit with small children. They laugh at me.' "Are you prepared to learn out of school"? He replied, 'Yes, provided I also earn'. "What type of job you want"? He said, "I would like to work in silk industry. I have some experience. It is paying".

CHAPTER III

Educational Status

The importance of education for development has been underscored in all the Five Year Plans as well as many research studies. Every segment of the population should receive attention and participate in educational programmes. If some sections do not participate, such groups become a liability to the Nation besides perpetuating backwardness among themselves.

The importance given for education in the Five Year Plans is summarised as "Educational expenditures promote the development of human resources. In the case of Backward Classes and Minorities in particular, apart from improving their skills and capabilities, educational outlays act as a powerful instrument for bringing about reduction in income inequalities".[1] The State has recognised the importance of education at the Pre-primary and Primary school levels. Education for the adults in general and women in particular has also been stressed during

1. Karnataka Draft Five Year Plan (1978-83) Planning Department, Government of Karnataka, p. 117.

all the plan periods. Importance of education for development has been focussed by many scholars.

Hall and Lauwers[1] observe that education is the instrument by which a Nation transforms itself from what it is into what it hopes to be. Carl stresses the need for social mobility through education. He observes that "when the school differentiates students early in their educational career, it is denying to those who are allocated to inferior status the only opportunity they have for social mobility"[2]

Islam has encouraged education for both men and women. Knowledge has been given due consideration for the progress of human beings in general and Muslims in particular. But there are abundant instances where we notice that Muslim society has deviated from this prescription of Islam. The available limited studies indicate that Muslims have remained socially backward because of educational backwardness. Emperical evidences cited in the work of the author in a recent study bear testimony to this.[3]

It is generally admitted that values of education have been hardly realised and encouraged in Muslim society. Even where people have accumulated wealth, education is not proportionately encouraged. Among the poor, particularly the labour class, increased income has not led to increased values of education. Further, even where values are recognised, very little has been done to practise them.

The status of education among Muslims in the present study covers adults and children. As said earlier, both these target

1. R.K. Hall and J.K. Lauwers, 'Education and Economics'. The Year Book of Education 1956, London, Evans Brokers, 1956, P. XI.
2. Carl Weinberg, 'Education and Social Problems', The Free Press, New York, Collier—Macmillan Ltd., London, 1971, p. 46.
3. Khan, Mumtaz Ali, 'Muslims in the Process of Rural Development in India,' Delhi : Uppal Publishing House, 1984.

groups are equally important for the development of Muslims. While adult education is needed to enable the participation of a large section of the population in development, education of the children is all the more important because Muslim society is facing acute problems from the deviant children by and large.

State has set up a number of Urdu schools at the Primary level and almost all the villages do have such schools. But whether the conditions of the schools are conductive to the children ? Whether the children are taking advantage of the facilities ? What is the response of the parents and the community ? Similarly, whether Muslim adults are participating in non-formal educational programmes ? If not, what are the hurdles ? What could be the possible solution to ensure their participation in these programmes ? These are some of the issues discussed in the present Chapter.

Educational Status of Respondents

Table 3.1 deals with the educational status of the respondents. Though there is not much difference between the number of literates and illiterates, the latter have a marginal edge over the former. While illiterates in general account for 52%, li terates are 48%.

Area wise presentation reveals significant differences. While 65% respondents in the North Karnataka region are illiterates, 42% are illiterates in Old Mysore. It means, the majority are literates in Old Mysore, whereas a vast majority are illiterates in North Karnataka, percentages being 58% and 64% respectively. This significant gap speaks for the relative backwardness of North Karnataka Muslims.

As literacy by itself does not convey the real and purposeful meaning, a break up of the levels of literacy would be more meaningful. Among the literates, the general position is that

TABLE 3.1

Educational Status of Respondents

Educational Status	*Old Mysore Area*		*North Karnataka Area*		*Total*	
	N	%	*N*	%	*N*	%
A. Literacy Status						
Illiteracy	176	42.3	198	64.7	374	51.8
Literacy	240	57.7	108	35.3	348	48.2
Total	416	100.0	306	100.0	722	100.0
B. Break up of literacy						
Lower primary	100	41.6	58	53.7	158	45.4
Upper primary	110	45.8	34	31.4	144	41.4
High school	16	6.6	12	11.1	28	8.1
Diploma in Technical Education	2	1.0	2	1.9	4	1.1
College	12	5.0	2	1.9	14	4.0
Total	240	100.0	108	100.0	348	100.0

87% have had only primary education. Those who are of lower primary status are slightly more than those who are of upper primary level. High school education is confined to only 8% of respondents. Higher education is virtually negligible.

Though the trend is similar in both areas, more educational backwardness is visible in North Karnataka where a higher percentage of respondents have primary education. However, in both the areas the majority have only reached the primary level (87% and 85%). Another feature is that while 54% respondents have studied upto lower primary standard and 31% upto upper primary level in North Karnataka area, there are more respondents with upper primary than lower primary in Old Mysore area (46% and 42%). Another feature is that higher education has more attraction in Old Mysore than in North Karnataka.

Types of Illiterates

As seen in Table 3.2, there are two categories of illiterates, namely original illiterate and relapsed or reverted illiterates among the respondents. In general, 53% are original illiterates and 47% are reverted illiterates.

When analysed in relation to the two areas, there is a significant difference between the two. While in Old Mysore 57% are original illiterates, it is 49% in North Karnataka. But, there are more relapsed illiterates in North Karnataka than in Old Mysore, the percentages being 51% and 43% respectively.

This difference would mean that children have no opportunity for continuous education after they drop-out. Facilities and motivation are generally missing. Respondents expressed their views regarding the reasons for this situation. They had to drop out early and take up jobs. They had no one to think of their educational needs after leaving the schools at an early

TABLE 3.2

Types of Illiterates Among Respondents

Types	*Old Mysore Area*		*North Karnataka Area*		*Total*	
	N	%	*N*	%	*N*	%
Original illiterates	100	56.8	97	49.0	197	52.7
Relapsed illiterates	76	43.2	101	51.0	177	47.3
Total	176	100.0	198	100.0	374	100.0

age. They too had not realised its importance. They feel that they could have continued to be in touch with their school books or newspapers, etc.

Drop-outs

'Drop-outs' constitute a major set-back to our educational programmes and policies. 'Drop-outs' among Muslims are also said to be a major problem. This is examined with the help of data furnished in Table 3.3.

A little more than 60% of respondents dropped out of schools in their early days. There is a higher percentage of drop-outs among the Muslims of Old Mysore (70%) than North Karnataka (60%). This is, of course, significantly different when compared to the general trend. In all the other areas of educational problems, the Old Mysore area is seen to be slightly better than the North Karnataka Area.

However, when we examine the levels at which drop-outs occur, it is seen that in North Karnataka there is a higher percentage of drop-outs at the lower primary level than in the Old Mysore area. But at the Upper primary level, there is a higher percentage in Old Mysore. What is significant is that a little more than 94% respondents dropped out at the primary level and only a negligible number went to High school in both the areas.

Reasons for Drop-outs

The reasons for drop-outs were discussed with the respondents in group situation. It was found that the major reason was poverty. Poverty was again the result of poor economic conditions as well as the large size of the families. Respondents do admit that if certain amount of pressure and motivation had been put, things could have been slightly different. When asked to comment on the issue that poverty is a common factor even among the Hindus, the consensus emerged was that

TABLE 3.3

Drop Outs Among the Respondents

Drop out level	*Old Mysore Area*		*North Karnataka Area*		*Total*	
	N	*%*	*N*	*%*	*N*	*%*
Lower primary	166	58.9	138	72.2	304	64.2
Upper primary	104	36.9	43	22.5	147	31.1
High school	12	4.2	10	5.3	22	4.7
Total	282	100.0	191	100.0	473	100.0

it was true. But among the Hindus in general there is a greater degree of awareness of the importance of education and efforts being made. But according to the respodents, Muslims take this as an excuse. 'We have money for every thing, but not for education. We have to blame ourselves'. This was how a few knowledgeable persons reacted.

Fducation and Occupation

The popular notion as well as the findings of a number of research studies indicate that lack of education besides levels of education depends upon the occupational status of the family. If the occupational background is encouraging, children receive better education. Similarly, if the occupational status is lower, children's education suffers. It was felt desirable to test this correlation in the present study. Table 3.4 has data on the educational status of the respondents in relation to occupational pattern. Both literacy status and levels of literacy are examined in relation to intra-occupational pattern.

Intra-occupational analysis indicates that there are more literates (53.4%) than illiterates among the cultivators (46.6%). But among the agricultural labourers, there are more illiterates (61.5%) than literates (38.5%). Similarly, among the industrial labourers as well as businessmen, there are more illiterates than literates. While the illiterates among industrial labourers account for 60.4%, it is 68% among the businessmen. Among those who are involved in industry and tailoring there are more literates than illiterates (66.7% and 56.4%).

Intra-occupational group analysis in relation to educational levels is presented here.

So far as levels of literacy among cultivators are concerned, 58.8% have only upto lower primary standard and 39.2% upto upper primary standard. It means that almost all these respondents have studied only upto primary standard. Only 2% have had high school education among the cultivators. Among the farm labourers, a vast majority are the those who had

TABLE 3.4

Educational Status of Respondents in Relation to occupation

Occupation	A. Educat onal Status					
	Illiteracy		Literacy		Total	
	N	%	N	%	N	%
1	2	3	4	5	6	7
Cultivation	89	46.6	102	53.4	191	100.0
Agricultural labour	99	61.5	62	38.5	161	100.0
Industry	6	33.3	12	66.7	18	100.0
Industrial labour	29	60.4	19	39.6	48	100.0
Government service	—	—	40	100.0	40	100.0
Business	105	67.7	50	32.3	155	100.0
Tailoring	24	44.4	31	56.4	55	100.0
Miscellaneous	8	66.7	4	33.3	12	100.0

B. Break up of Levels of Literacy

Lower Primary		Upper Primary		High School		College		Total	
N	%	*N*	%	*N*	%	*N*	%	*N*	%
8	9	10	11	12	13	14	15	16	17
60	58.8	40	39.2	2	2.0	—	—	102	100.0
50	80.6	12	19.4	—	—	—	—	62	100.0
4	33.3	8	66.7	—	—	—	—	12	100.0
12	63.2	7	36.8	—	—	—	—	19	100.0
2	5.0	18	45.0	14	35.0	6	15.0	40	100.0
18	36.0	28	56.0	4	8.0	—	—	50	100.0
10	32.3	17	54.8	4	12.9	—	—	31	100.0
—	—	4	100.0	—	—	—	—	4	100.0

studied upto lower primary standard (80.6%) and the rest have upper primary education. There is none having high school education.

Among those involved in industries, there none having studies beyond upper primary level. Two-thirds of them have had upper primary education (66.7%) and one-third lower primary education. Among the industrial labourers, there is a larger number having lower primary (63.2%) than upper primary (36.8%). There is none beyond upper primary. Among those who are in Government service, those who have studied upto upper primary and beyond upper primary are almost equal in number (45% and 50%). But those who had only upto lower primary are extremely marginal (5%). There are some with college education too (15%).

Among the respondents involved in business and tailoring, a vast majority have studied only upto primary standard (92% and 87%) with more in upper primary than lower primary (56% and 55% repectively).

It is thus obvious that generally more illiterates as well as as those who had lower primary education are among the manual labourers. There is clear link between levels of literacy and the occupational status.

Education and Income

Just as there could be correlation between education and occupational status, popular view is that educational status depends upon income. Research studies also indicate this trend generally. Is this true among Muslims too ? It is just seen that there is linkage between education and occupational status among Muslims too. The position in relation to income is analysed with the help of data presented in table 3.5.

Intra-income group anlysis provides a better picture. Among those who have lower income, a vast majority are illiterates

TABLE 3.5

Educational Levels of Respondents in Relation to Income

Income	A. Educational Status				Total	
	Illiteracy		Literacy			
	N	%	*N*	%	*N*	%
1	2	3	4	5	6	7
Low Income	300	69.1	134	30.9	434	100.0
Mid Income (Rs. 300—600)	59	32.2	124	67.8	183	100.0
High Income (600+)	15	14.3	90	85.7	105	100.0

B. Break up of Levels of Literacy

Lower Primary		*Upper Primary*		*High School*		*College*		*Total*	
N	%	*N*	%	*N*	%	*N*	%	*N*	%
8	9	10	11	12	13	14	15	16	17
95	70.9	35	26.1	4	3.0	—	—	134	100.0
53	42.7	57	46.0	8	6.4	6	4.8	124	100.0
10	11.1	52	57.8	16	17.8	12	13.3	90	100.0

(69.1%). Among those placed, in middle income group, majority are literates (67.8%). This is also the position among those who have high income (85.7%).

When levels of literacy are examined with reference to Low income, it is seen that almost all have had only upto primary education (97%), with lower primary level accounting for 70.9%. Those who had high school education are extremely insignificant.

In middle income group, even though the majority had primary education (88.7%), there are more with upper primary education (46.0%) than with lower primary education. There are also 6.4% of respondents having education in high school and 4.8% college education.

In the higher income range, the position is very much different. Even though the vast majority have primary education (68.9%), it is seen that those who have upper primary level are in greater number with 57.8% than those having lower primary education (11.1%). The gap is quite significant here than in the case of mid-income range. Further, the number of persons having high school (17.8%) and college (13.3%) education is much more than in the case of mid-income group.

It is thus evident here that educational status is related to income. Higher the income better is educational status. The relation between income and education is more significant than the relation between occupation and education.

Literacy Among Children

The literacy status among the children is presented in table 3.6. In general, a little more than half of the children are literates (51%). This percentage is no doubt quite encouraging, but the real situation gets manifested when an attempt is made to find out the levels of literacy. This exercise is done a little later. The position in relation to sex of the child is a little

TABLE 3.6

Literacy Status Among Children

Literacy Status	Old Mysore Area					
	Males		Females		Total	
	N	%	N	%	N	%
1	2	3	4	5	6	7
Literates	346	51.95	390	60.84	736	56.31
Illiterates	320	48.05	251	39.16	571	43.69
Total	666	100.0	641	100.0	1307	100.0

North Karnataka Area						Total					
Male		Female		Total		Male		Female		Total	
N	%	N	%	N	%	N	%	N	%	N	%
8	9	10	11	12	13	14	15	16	17	18	19
190	45.24	170	41.46	360	43.37	536	49.36	560	53.28	1096	51.29
230	54.76	240	58.54	470	56.63	550	50.64	491	46.72	1041	48.71
420	100.00	410	100.00	830	100.00	1086	100.00	1051	100.00	2137	100.00

more interesting. Normally, we except higher percentage of literates among the boys. But in the present study it is seen that female children account for a slightly higher percentage. While literacy among the male children is to the extent of 49%, it is 53% in the case of the girls. It means that 51% are illiterates among the boys while it is below 50% among the girls.

What could be the possible reasons for this situation. The data indicate this. It is because of the varying situations in the two areas. In the Old Mysore area, though the majority of the male children as well as female children are literates, female children are more in number. While the boys account for 52% of literacy, it is 61% among the girls. But the situation is very much different in the North Karnataka area where illiteracy is to a larger extent among boys as well as girls. While 55% boys are illiterates, 59% girls are illiterates. To sum up, while 56% children are literates in Old Mysore area, 56% are illiterates in North Karnataka area.

Literacy Levels

As said earlier, levels of literacy make all the difference in the educational advancement of the children. This is particularly so among the rural poor. One of the factors that enables vertical social mobility is the standard of education received by the child. This situation is analysed in the present study.

Table 3.7 relates to the literacy levels of children. In general, it is seen that a vast majority of children accounting for as high as 89% have had only primary education. A further probe would mean that even here lower primary standard has an upper hand. The gap between the lower primary and the upper primary standards is quite significant. While 55% had only lower primary education, only 34% are with upper primary School standard.

Among boys and girls in general, the situation is no better

TABLE 3.7

Literacy Levels among Children

Levels of Literacy	*Old Mysore Area*					
	Male		*Female*		*Total*	
	N	%	*N*	%	*N*	%
1	2	3	4	5	6	7
Lower Primary	160	46.24	229	58.72	389	52.85
Upper Primary	120	34.68	130	33.33	250	33.97
High School	56	16.18	31	7.95	87	11.82
College	10	2.90	—	—	10	1.36
Total	346	100.0	390	100.0	736	100.0

North Karnataka Area						*Total*					
Male		*Female*		*Total*		*Male*		*Female*		*Total*	
N	%	N	%	N	%	N	%	N	%	N	%
8	9	10	11	12	13	14	15	16	17	18	19
110	57.89	100	58.82	210	58.33	270	50.37	329	58.75	599	54.65
58	30.53	64	37.65	122	33.89	178	33.21	194	34.64	372	33.94
20	10.53	6	3.53	26	7.22	76	14.18	37	6.61	113	10.31
2	1.05	—	—	2	0.56	12	2.24	—	—	12	1.10
190	100.0	170	100.0	360	100.0	536	100.0	560	100.0	1096	100.0

excepting that among girls there are more with lower primary school standard (50%) as against the boys (50%). At the upper primary level, there is only a marginal difference. But so far as high school education is concerned, the gap between the boys and girls is too wide. While 14% boys are in high school, only 7% girls are here. Further, while 12 boys are in college, none of the girls are in college.

The position is more or less similar in both the areas excepting in the case of boys. It is seen that while 46% boys are in lower primary in Old Mysore area, it is 58% in North Karnataka. A similar difference is found with regard to high school standard. However, among girls of these two areas, there is a virtual similarity with certain marginal variations.

Types of illiterates

The types of illiterates among the children are presented in table 3.8. The two types discussed earlier in relation to the respondents are original illiteracy and reverted illiteracy. Original illiteracy accounts for 57%, whereas relapsed illiteracy to the extent of 43%. This general position holds good in the case of boys as well as girls. The trend is similar between boys and girls, though a slightly higher percentage of original illiteracy is noticed among boys (58%), whereas girls account for a slightly higher percentage of reverted illiterates (45%).

When viewed from the angle of the two regions, it is noticed that both boys and girls account for a higher percentage of original illiterates in both the areas, whereas girls account for a slightly higher percentage of relapsed illiterates.

The two major features of this analysis are that illiteracy is still a major problem and relapsed illiteracy is quite significant. The various reasons advanced for this situation are that when children drop-out of schools, generally after primary IV standard, they get involved in domestic work and have hardly

TABLE 3.8

Types of Illiterates among the Children

Types of Illiterates	*Old Mysore Area*					
	Males		*Females*		*Total*	
	N	*%*	*N*	*%*	*N*	*%*
1	2	3	4	5	6	7
Original	180	56.25	140	55.78	320	56.04
Relapsed	140	43.75	111	44.22	251	43.96
Total	320	100.00	251	100.00	571	100.00

North Karnataka Area						Total					
Males		Females		Total		Males		Females		Total	
N	%	N	%	N	%	N	%	N	%	N	%
8	9	10	11	12	13	14	15	16	17	18	19
140	60.87	130	54.17	270	57.45	320	58.18	270	54.99	590	56.68
90	39.13	110	45.83	200	42.55	230	41.82	221	45.01	451	43.32
230	100.00	240	100.00	470	100.00	550	100.00	491	100.00	1041	100.00

any scope or facility for continuing education. The second feature is that there is less original illiteracy among girls is north Karnataka (54%) when compared to boys (61%).

Reasons for Illiteracy

Respondents assign various reasons for illiteracy among the children. This position is presented in table 3.9. The eight reasons are : lack of interest among the children, financial problems, early jobs, influence of others, lack of motivation, lack of Urdu schools, lack of separate schools for girls and domestic work.

In general, 15% respondents feel that the children do not have interest in attending schools. They were not able to say something definite as to why children lack interest. The only answer given is that inspite of the best efforts of the parents, some children are incorrigible. This is so in both the areas, though a little higher percentage is seen in North Karnataka.

Finance seems to be the real crux of the problem. This accounts for 28% in general. In between the Old Mysore and North Karnataka areas, the former has more respondents assigning this reason. What would really constitute the financial problems ? Whether education is so expensive that the parents cannot afford to spend some amount on children's education ? When these issues were discussed in small groups, some light was thrown.

Two reasons were advanced. First, some parents take children's education so lightly that they do not bother to know if there was any real difficulty in educating their children. Rural schools are still managed by the Government and therefore, the question of monthly fee and other expenses would not arise. The second reason which appears to be relevant is the fact the parents have a tendency to send the children for work so that they earn a little and this limited income is something very much needed to run the family.

TABLE 3.9

Reasons for Illiteracy

Reasons	*Old Mysore Area*		*North Karnataka Area*		*Total*	
	N	*%*	*N*	*%*	*N*	*%*
Lack of Interest among children	58	13.94	10	16.34	108	14.96
Financial problems	130	31.25	72	23.53	202	27.98
Early jobs	40	9.62	32	10.46	72	9.97
Influence of others	25	6.01	24	7.84	49	6.79
Lack of Motivation	30	7.21	24	7.84	54	7.47
Lack of Urdu schools	25	6.01	16	5.23	41	5.68
Lack of separate schools for girls	50	12.02	40	13.07	90	12.47
Domestic work	58	13.94	48	15.69	106	14.68
Total	416	100.0	306	100.00	722	100.00

Domestic work is another important reason. Nearly 15% respondents assign this reason in general. This is also the position in both the areas. Domestic work would include helping mother in kitchen and other house hold management works. Most of the female children are involved in this work.

Lack of separate schools for girls is considered to be an important reason by 12% respondents in general which is also true in both the areas. There is a tendency among the Muslim parents to observe certain cultural restrictions while providing education to their girls. Even if they are not against education for girls, quite often they do not favour girls sitting in common class rooms among the boys, particularly after the sixth standard by which time girls would have attained puberty.

When asked as to how Hindu parents send their female children to common schools, the Muslim respondents would just say 'it all depends upon the philosophy of their religion. Islam would not permit such common sitting'. Respondents would not be convinced by any other reason.

The other reasons are :

(1) the desire to seek early jobs by the boys. This is to the extent of 10% in general and a similar trend in the two areas ;

(2) It is also said that there are some boys and girls who bring pressure directly and indirectly on some children who would have gone to schools but for this influence.

Parents feel that this pressure at an early age is likely to disturb the mind of the children who would be tempted to keep themselves away from the schools and spend a happy time.

The third reason is lack of proper motivation accounted for by 7% respondents in general as well as in the two areas. Parents admit that they could not convince the children. If some people from outside could take up this social work, children could perhaps be motivated to join school. Some body who is educated and who holds better status should come forward, according to the parents.

Lack of Urdu schools in some villages is another reason, though not very significant. About 6% respondents say so. They do not want their children to join Kannada schools. The position is similar in both the areas. The fear expressed is that 'Islamic culture' gets damaged and influenced by the 'Hindu culture'. When pointed out that in some States like Kerala and Tamil Nadu Muslim children attend Malayalam and Tamil medium schools, the respondents gave evasive answers either out of ignorance or wrong notions.

When the parents' attention was drawn to the fact that even Muslims in urban areas have started sending their children to English medium schools and why in such cases objections are not raised, rural Muslims would just say 'we do not know. May be urban Muslims are really not so much bothered about Muslim culture'.

Drop-Outs Among Children

The 'drop-outs' pattern in both Old Mysore and North Karnataka regions is presented in table 3.10. There are in all 1,241 childred who have dropped out of schools. These dropouts are limited to primary school, both lower and upper primary.

In Old Mysore area there are 876 dropouts. Among them, there are 446 (50.9%) male children and 430 (49.1%) female children. The difference between them is too narrow. But the situation is different in North Karnataka region. In this region, there are 204 (55.9%) boys and 161 (44.1%) girls who have dropped out. This would mean that the number of dropouts is more in the case of boys than in the case of girls.

TABLE 3.10

Position of Drop Outs among Children

Area	*Males*		*Females*		*Total*	
	N	%	*N*	%	*N*	%
Old Mysore Area	446	50.9	430	49.1	876	100.0
North Karnataka Area	204	55.9	161	44.1	365	100.0
Total	650	52.4	591	47.6	1241	100.0

Reasons for Drop-outs

Various reasons are advanced by the respondents for drop-out among the children as seen in table 3.11. Financial problems, lack of parental interest, co-education, male teacher and poor quality of teachers constitute these major reasons. Of these reasons, the general situation is that 38% respondents give financial problem as the major reason, followed by 25% giveng poor quality teachers, In between are the other reasons. While 18% say lack of parental interest is the reason, co-education and male teacher are to the extent of 11% and 7% respectively.

The general situation in relation to the boys and girls is that financial position gets the first place among the boys and girls. But while among the boys poor quality of teachers gets the second place, it gets the third place among the girls. Co-education gets the second place among the girls. Parents are very much averse to the girls being taught by the male teachers. In fact, it is seen that the girls drop-out after primary standard mostly because of this. A further probe reveals that it is not religions per se that comes in the way. Muslims feel that their culture does not permit them free mixing of girls with the boys.

There are some similarities and differences between the boys and girls in Old Mysore and North Karnataka areas. In Old Mysore area, financial problems and poor quality of teachers account for about 40% each in the case of the boys. But in North Karnataka, 54% respondents give financial problem as the major reason and only 17% say poor quality teacher. In North Karnataka, 29% say that lack of parental interest is the factor in the case of boys.

So far as girls are concerned, it is seen that the pattern is more or less similar between the two areas excepting in regard to lack of parental control as the reason. While 19% in North Karnataka advance this reason, it is only to the extent of 9%

TABLE 3.11

Reasons for Drop-out

Reasons	*Old Mysore Area*					
	Males		*Females*		*Total*	
	N	*%*	*N*	*%*	*N*	*%*
1	2	3	4	5	6	7
Financial problems	176	39.5	140	32.6	316	36.1
Lack of parental interest	90	20.1	40	9.3	130	14.8
Co-education	—	—	100	23.3	100	11.4
Male teacher	—	—	70	16.2	70	8.0
Poor quality teachers	180	40.4	80	18.6	260	29.7
Total	446	100.0	430	100.0	876	100.0

North Karnataka Area						Total					
Males		*Females*		*Total*		*Males*		*Females*		*Total*	
N	%	*N*	%	*N*	%	*N*	%	*N*	%	*N*	%
8	9	10	11	12	13	14	15	16	17	18	19
110	53.9	50	31.1	160	43.8	286	44.0	190	32.1	476	38.3
60	29.4	31	19.3	91	24.9	150	23.0	71	12.0	221	17.8
—	—	40	24.8	40	11.0	—	—	140	23.7	140	11.3
—	—	20	12.4	20	5.5	—	—	90	15.2	90	7.3
34	16.7	20	12.4	54	14.8	214	33.0	100	17.0	314	25.3
204	100.0	161	100.0	365	100.0	650	100.0	591	100.0	1241	100.0

in Old Mysore area. There are, of course, minor differences between the two areas in regard to other reasons.

Types and Levels of Education Needed

Two types of education have been taken up for consideration. These are secular education and theological education. Within each type, levels of education desired are also examined. The data are presented in table 3.12.

Secular Education

It is seen that in general, 58% desire beyond upper primary level. While 34% want high school standard, 23% need college education. The remaining 42% are content with primary education. But here more respondents (33%) desire upper primary level than lower primary.

The respondents in the two regions have certain amount of differences in their opinion. While in both the areas, only a small number is content with lower primary standard, more respondents of North Karnataka area desire upper primary than those in Old Mysore area. This would mean that there is a larger number in Old Mysore area needing education beyond upper primary level than those in North Karnataka area. In particular, this is so in regard to college education (26%) and (20% respectively).

Theological Education

So far as theological education is concerned, in general it is noticed that 89% desire basic standard and only 11% desire proficiency. The position is identical in both the regions. The Muslim mind was revealed more clearly in group disussions. Every one realised and expressed the view that religious knowledge is needed for progress and peace. Islamic theological studies are essential.

TABLE 3.12

Types and Levels of Education Desired

Types and Level of Education	Old Mysore Area N	Old Mysore Area %	North Karnataka Area N	North Karnataka Area %	Total N	Total %
A. Secular						
Lower primary	40	9.6	30	9.8	70	9.7
Upper primary	120	28.9	115	37.6	235	32.6
High school	146	35.1	101	33.0	247	34.2
College Education	110	26.4	60	19.6	170	23.5
Total	416	100.0	306	100.0	722	100.0
B. Theological						
Basic	370	88.9	270	88.2	640	88.6
Proficiency	46	11.1	36	11.8	82	11.4
Total	416	100.0	306	100.0	722	100.0

But the difference was upto what level. People were almost unanimous that the proficiency level is desired by those who could become priests and religious leaders. For others basic knowledge would be adequate. If every one become proficient in Islamic studies at the cost of general education, then the future of such a person could be a problem. People today depend upon secular education for their livelihood. But they also realise that religious education is equally important. But a basic and clear knowledge could be adequate besides the general education.

The Need for Primary Education

Though primary education seems to be in general the need of the hour in view of the Constitutional provision for free and compulsory education between the sixth and the fourteenth year of the child, the general trend is to allow children only upto primary standard and withdraw thereafter. Why parents need primary education ? What benefits they anticipate out of this education ? Is there any difference in the attitudes of the parents towards the need for boys and girls ? These are some of the important and interesting issues discussed with the help of the data presented in table 3.13.

There are six reasons assigned by the respondents. These are: jobs, security, letter-writing, reading stories, reading religious books and help in work. In otherwords, these are the expected advantages that flow out of primary education if given to the children.

There is not much significant difference between the respondents of Old Mysore area and North Karnataka area in general. In both these areas there seems to be uniformity in the opinion of the respondents both in the case of boys and girls. There is some variation in the percentages, but not of much significance. But what is really significant is the attitude of the respondents towards the girls. While 16.6% respondent, desire primary

TABLE 3.13

Need for Primary Education

Reason	Old Mysore Area			
	For Males		For Females	
	N	%	*N*	%
1	2	3	4	5
Job	70	16.8	16	3.8
Security	66	15.9	98	23.6
Letter writing	70	16.8	80	19.2
Reading stories	76	18.3	66	15.9
Reading religious books	64	15.4	76	18.3
Help in work	70	16.8	80	19.2
Total	416	100.0	416	100.0

North Karnataka Area				Total			
For Males		For Females		For Males		For Females	
N	%	N	%	N	%	N	%
6	7	8	9	10	11	12	13
50	16.3	12	3.9	120	16.6	28	3.9
46	15.0	88	28.8	110	15.5	186	25.8
60	19.7	60	19.6	130	18.1	140	19.4
62	20.2	46	15.0	138	19.1	112	15.5
40	13.1	70	22.9	104	14.4	146	20.2
48	15.7	30	9.8	118	16.3	110	15.2
306	100.0	306	100.0	722	100.0	722	100.0

education for boys to enable them to get jobs, only 3.9% respondents desire this for girls. The second important difference is in relation to security. While 15.5% respondents desire primary education for boys for security purpose, 25.8% them desire it for girls. It means that social security in times of unexpected changes in the family is a very important concern of the parents for their daughters. In group discussion, a vast majority of them said that after marriage, if some confflicts arise between the husbands and wives which might lead to divorce or desertation, then the daughters would be in danger. This is also because of the fear of the daughters becoming widows.

In such tragic situations, parents feel that even primary education might help the daughters to stand on their own strength. They might get some jobs. They would have confidence. They can think well and do something that would enable them to eke out their living.

Need for Higher Education

The need for higher education seems to be different from the need for primary education as seen in Table 3.14. Five reasons are given for higher education. In general, higher education for jobs gets top consideration. Nearly 50% of the respondents do feel so in favour of males. Even in the case of females, education is needed for jobs, according to 29% of respondents. While acquisition of knowledge gets the second place in the case of male children, security finds the second place in the case of the females. Status gets the third place for males, whereas adjustment in life gets the third place for females.

This would mean that though higher education is needed for both the males and the females, the reasons for this vary significantly. Higher education for women is for jobs, social security and adjustment in life, whereas for males more emphasis is given for jobs and status.

TABLE 3.14

Need for Higher Education

Reasons	Old Mysore Area			
	For Males		For Females	
	N	%	N	%
1	2	3	4	5
Jobs	198	47.6	130	31.2
Knowledge	80	19.2	70	16.8
Status	70	16.9	46	11.1
Security	38	9.1	98	23.6
Adjustment in life	30	7.2	72	17.3
Total	416	100.0	416	100.0

North Karnataka Area				Total			
For Males		*For Females*		*For Males*		*For Females*	
N	%	*N*	%	*N*	%	*N*	%
6	7	8	9	10	11	12	13
159	52.0	79	25.9	357	49.5	209	28.9
50	16.4	46	15.0	130	18.0	116	16.1
40	13.0	36	11.8	110	15.2	82	11.4
30	9.8	76	24.8	68	9.4	174	24.1
27	8.8	69	22.5	57	7.9	141	19.5
306	100.0	306	100.0	722	100.0	722	100.0

This general trend is more or less similar in both the areas. However, in the case of education for females, there is some significant difference in relation to jobs and adjustment in life. A higher percentage of respondent in the Old Mysore area than in North Karnataka feel that higher education for females is needed for jobs. Similarly, there is greater emphasis on higher education for females for adjustment in life in North Karnataka than in the Old Mysore area.

Thus, it is noticed that though both primary and higher educational levels are desired by the respondents for both males and females, reasons given for such education for males and females differ to a large extent. Female education is considered for social security, jobs and adjustment in life whereas education for males is generally for jobs and status in society.

Problems of Education

The status of literacy, drop-outs and reasons for the poor performance, etc. have been examined earlier. There is another interesting and important aspect of educational advancement among the poor in particular. Whether these poor people are conscious of these problems which affect the progress of education, directly or indirectly. Hence, this issue was also taken up in the present study.

Views of the respondents are presented in table 3.15. Six reasons are advanced. In general, 'irregular teachers' is the most important reason. Nearly one-fourth of the respondents have expressed their views that if the teachers are not regular in their work and attendance, how could children receive good education? They aired their grievances by giving concrete instances. "Teachers stay quite often outside the place of school. They come late and leave early because of bus convenience. Teachers do not have that commitment. Muslim teachers are very bad. They have no concern. They know how to receive fat salary". These were some of the adverse remarks

TABLE 3.15

Problem of Education

Problems	*Old Mysore Area* N	*Old Mysore Area* %	*North Karnataka Area* N	*North Karnataka Area* %	*Total* N	*Total* %
Poor Buildings	62	14.9	52	17.0	114	15.8
Irregular teachers	98	23.6	79	25.8	177	24.6
Lack of good facilities	72	17.3	55	18.0	127	17.6
Lack of control over teachers	76	18.3	60	19.6	136	18.8
Lack of interest among parents	28	6.7	20	6.5	48	6.6
Unemployment among the educated	80	19.2	40	13.1	120	16.6
Total	416	100.0	306	100.0	722	100.0

made by the respondents. This is also the situation in both the areas with slight difference in the percentages.

Lack of control over the teachers is another reason frequented by the resdondents. Nearly 19% say so Their contention is that the Inspectors of schools rarely visit the schools. Even when they visit they pretend to be strict. Some times they shout at the teachers. But very rarely they punish them. Teachers also know the game. Some knowledgeable respondents said "Sir, Inspectors and Head Masters are one. They are partners. Inspectors are nicely fed and entertained. Why should they bother about the children?"

Neither the parents have any type of controls over the teachers. The fact that a vast majority of the parents are illiterates and ignorant helps the deviant teachers. Betterment committees are almost defunct and even where they exist, no purpose is served.

In contrast, some of the respondents point out that the Kannada medium schools are much better. There is some discipline. Teachers take more interest. The regularity of the teachers is assured. Examinations are properly conducted. There is a tendency among the Muslim parents to send their children to Kannada medium schools. A few instances of much significance were quoted. In some families, one child would go to Kannada medium and the other to Urdu medium schools. Parents point out the differences in the behaviour of the children, their responses and performance.

Nearly 33% respondents said that lack of facilities and buildings would also amount to a sort of hurdle for smooth progress of children's education. There were buildings shown to the research workers. These buildings were in most dangerous conditions. Roofs would pose potential danger. Windows have no shutters. During rainy season, there would be leakage and the class rooms would be full of water. In some places toilet facilities are not to be found. Respondents feel that Urdu schools are given step-motherly treatment by the State.

Unemployment among the educated is no doubt a general problem facing all sections of the society. In the present study, 17% respondents say 'why should we educate our children beyond primary education? If they become matriculates and graduates, they will not go to the farm. They develop different attitudes towards work ethics. They want jobs in Government but Government does not give jobs.

Admission Age and Enrolment

Age at which a child is admitted has some significance. It reflects the awareness of the age factor and the response to it. Normally there are two categories of age at which a child can be admitted to the primary school. First is 5+ and secondly 5 + 10. Under voluntary admission a child who has completed 5 years can be enrolled by the school authorities. Under Compulsory Education Act, every child who has completed 5+10 should be admitted by the parents.

The basic problem as revealed in the study is that the majority of the parents are not aware of both the age groups. Still worse is the fact that they do not remember the date of birth of the chidren. They do not have documentary evidence even through the law requires this. What the parents do is that they take the children to the school and ask the teacher to enrol the child. It was also brought to the notice the research team that some of them know the census conducted in December every year to take stock of eligible children for enrolment.

Since the parents could not give information on the age at which their children were admitted to school both under voluntary and compulsory admission, the school teachers had to be approached. According to the information received from them, not more than 10% children got admitted on voluntary basis in

Old Mysore area and it was below 8% in North Karnataka area. They were all male children. In other words, no female child got admitted on voluntary basis. When asked the parents said that the wanted boys to be admitted as early as possible, not girls. "There is no such a hurry to admit young girls to school", said some parents.

Enrolment

Enrolment drive undertaken by the teachers of the Government schools has had great impact. During the last five years in particular, parents have responded well. As a result of this, nearly 80% children had been admitted. There was a higher percentage of boys than girls. Further, the situation was more or less similar in both the areas.

Still parents encounter some problem in getting their childern admitted. Either children refuse to go or some parents lack interest unless they are motivated. Teachers also visit the families and try to tempt the children. But sometimes the children would not budge. The distance between the school and the residence poses a real problem.

Pre primary Education

Pre-primary education has assumed greater significance for various reasons. The four important reason are :

(1) it paves way for better socialization of children right form the early age,

(2) children are introduced into the world of learning at the early age through play,

(3) working mothers will have some relief, and

(4) elder children can attend to schools regularly instead of taking care of children at home.

There are two broad categories of pre-primary education, namely

(1) Integrated Child Development Scheme (ICDS) and

(2) Nursery schools.

While the former is Government sponsored and is still selective in its operational areas and population, the latter is mostly privately managed. Rural areas are generally not covered by the Nursery schools.

In the recent Five Year Plans, lot of importance is given for pre-primary education. To what extent the people are aware of this and whether they are interested and participating in this programme ? These issues were discussed with both respondents in general and selected knowledgeable persons. While the respondents in general expressed almost total ignorance of this scheme, the latter category had some knowledge. The general respondents when informed about the scheme, expressed their happiness and eagerness to participate in the programme. Most of them gave the reasons for their favourable opinion as expressed above. The knowledgeable Mulims expressed their dissatisfaction with the Government for not extending this important facility to them. When asked as to why some capable persons did not start such programmes, they felt that they would find it hard to run because money and teachers are required. But they would definitely take more interest in finding some solution to the problem.

This issue was further probed into with selected respondents in group discussions. Four suggestions were offered to them. First, two to three girls could be identified for training and these girls should have atleast upper primary education and aptitude. Secondly, they could be sent for training for a couple of weeks. Thirdly, they should not expect big salary and fourthly efforts should be made to explore financial assistance through local contribution and rich Muslims elsewhere.

There was favourable opinion in general. The only fear was about finances. These people had no hesitation to say that rich

Muslims would not come forward to help in educational matters and poor have no money to pay.

Conditions of Schools

Parents were sore over the utterly disgusting conditions of schools. They took the research team to some schools. A few instances are narrated here.

In Razack Palya, 14 miles from Bangalore City, the Government Urdu school presents a distressing situation. In one room there were two black boards on which whatever the teacher writes is not at all visible. There was a map of India in extremely bad shape, almost torn.

There were on roll 180 sudents from Primary I to VII. Boys and girls were more or less in equal number. Out of this number, 47 students had either left the school or were not attending school for a long time. The teachers were helpless in regular attendance. A large number of students did not attend the examinations. There was no seriousness at all.

There is a School Betterment Committee. No meetings were held eversince its formation three years ago. The Head Master would send meeting notices. But none would even bother to respond. The Head Master would feel bad and incur the displeasence of the locals if he ever tried to force the attendance of the members.

Teacher—parents relationship was highly explosive. Often they would quarrel. The teacher would try to force regularity and cleanliness among the students. But parents would feel bad. Some of them would even remark : "Should our boys and girls make up and come to the class room. Are you going to make them actors and actresses ?"

On one occasion the teacher tried to correct the erring student of II standard. The boy told the teacher, 'You come out, I shall see. You do not go to your house today'. The teacher got annoyed and beat the boy. Parents were approached. But they took the teacher to task instead of correcting the boy.

While teachers hold parents and village elders responsible for the growing indiscipline and irregularity, the parents would say, "What is it that we, illitrate parents, can do. If the teachers are regular and punctual and create interest, why our boys and girls do not go to schools. These teachers who come from Bangalore city are only interested in getting good salary. They come late and go early".

Case-study of Anwarrulla

A few cases of graduates were cited. These graduates are disillusioned. They sit in petty shops, repenting frequently for having gone to college. They feel sad and depressed. Their classmates are well settled in Government service. One interesting case-study is quoted here. In one of the villages, a graduate was contacted. He obtained his B.Sc. degree five years ago. He applied for quite a few jobs. He was called for an interview for the post of sub-Inspector of Police. The boy is quite sturdy and smart. He was asked to pay fifty thousand rupees by the way of illegal gratification to get the job. The middle man was requested to get the amount reduced. The boy told him 'My friend paid only twenty five thousand rupees and got the job. Why do you want me to pay more ? The middle man said 'You are short. To overcome this deficiency you have to pay double that amount.

The boy, Anwarulla, felt bad and said 'no'. He invested twenty-five thousand rupees on business and improvement of the small farm. He said 'Sir I am happy. I am living a decent and honest life. My income is not much. But it gives me satisfaction that it is my hard earned money. As a Police Officer I would have taken bribe and become anti-social element. Thank God, I am mentally happy. But I feel sorry for my parents who spent a lot on my education. They used to tell all the relatives that one day their son would become an officer. Today they are depressed".

Lack of interest among the parents is to the extent of 7%. "What our boys are going to do after their studies? Where is money with us to educate them? We have enough responsibility to get our daughters married". This is how some respondents would react.

Case-Study of Feroz Pasha

Feroz Pasha is 14 years old living in Razack Palya in Bangalore District. His father is a labourer employed by a silk merchant. He is illiterate. He has 10 children besides his wife and mother. His economic condition is very bad. Only 2 children are attending school in the village.

When asked why he did not send all his children to school, he just replied 'Sir, what can I do? I have a large family. My wife has to work at home and outside to earn some money. Young kids should be taken care of by the elder girls. I want my children to earn some amount daily'.

As the discussion was going on, Feroz Pasha appeared on the scene. He is the third child in the order of seniority. The conversation is as follows;

Self: Why did you not go to school today?

F.P.: Why today: Sir, I left the school 4 years ago.

Self: Why did you leave?

F.P.: My father wanted me to go to some silk reeler's house, work and bring money.

Self: How far did you study.

S.P.: Primary IV standard.

Self: Do you know reading and writing?

F.P.: No Sir, I have forgotten completely.

Self : How do you now feel for not going to school ?

F.P. : I feel ashamed. My friends who are going to school show their thumb to me and say 'you are this'. I did not understand this for some time. Then I asked some one what is the significance of this. I was informed that I am illiterate and have to use my thumb for whatever I receive. I feel sorry for leaving the school. I hold my father responsible for my illiteracy. My father is a drunkard. He wants money, money and only money. He forces my mother also to go out, work, earn and give him whatever she earns. My mother is a nice person. She is interested in our welfare. But she is helpless.

Self : What would have been your condition had you continued your studies ?

F.P. : Sir, I would have done SSLC and become either a teacher or a constable.

Adult Education

Non-formal education is considered to be one of the most important instruments to effect a certain amount of change among the illiterates who have passed the age of schooling and are involved in various types of work. It is here that adult education has to play a vital role. The Old Mysore State is said to be the earliest State in pre-Independent India for having launched adult education programmes on a mass scale.

Though this programme is expected to cover all adults, irrespective of religious and caste considerations, it is not popular among the Muslims. Very rarely do Muslims participate in it. There are various problems which effect their participation. The problems faced by the respondents are presented in Table 3.16.

TABLE 3.16

Problems of Adult Education

Problems	*Old Mysore Area*		*North Karnataka Area*		*Total*	
	N	%	*N*	%	*N*	%
Timings for convenient	101	24.3	101	33.0	202	28 0
Place not suitable	60	14.4	35	11.4	95	13.1
Contents not good for Muslims	89	21.4	60	19.7	149	20.6
People incharge are not good	86	20.7	70	22.9	156	21.7
Harmful to Muslim women	80	19.2	40	13.0	120	16.6
Total	416	100.0	306	100.0	722	100.0

There are five problems brought to light. These are : inconvenient timings, unsuitable places, unhelpful contents, unhelpful teachers in charge and harmful to Muslim women. In general, 28% Muslims feel that timings are not convenient. Adult education classes are conducted, if at all, in the evenings. During this period men and women will be busy. Women have to attend to domestic work and child care. Men will be busy with outside work. Moreover, this is prayer time.

Those who point out that the place is not suitable say that Muslim women in particular do not want to go to places outside their residential area as this is not permitted by their menfolk. Cultural constraints act as major deterrants. People who say so constitute 13%. Twenty-one per cent of respondents are not happy with the contents of the book. This is a very important factor from Muslims' point of view. Some of them argue that the contents are generally Hindu mythology-oriented. This would therefore not create much interest. A few respondents said that the contents are not useful for their daily socio-economic activities.

Twenty-two per cent of respondents expressed the view that people in charge of the programmes are not good. They are not helpful. Seventeen per cent respondents feel that the programme is harmful to Muslim women. Their main grouse is that often male teachers are incharge and therefore, Muslim women hesitate to go.

One significant factors that needs to be brought out here is that not all the Muslim respondents are educated and hence how could they offer their comments on various issues related to the programme. Muslim respondents are aware of this programme to a large extent, as pointed out somewhere else in the study. They have heard from others about the contents of the books and other problems. But they could give their opinion on other issues. But the group discussions with knowledgeable persons provided better insights. This would confirm the general feelings expressed by the respondents who are not educated but could still offer their comments.

Facilities Required

It is significant to note that the respondents are not averse to the need for adult education. No one questions its relevance. But the respondents expressed certain problems because of which their participation was not possible. They were then asked to indicate their needs so that they could also take advantage of the movement. They could offer five suggestions as seen in Table 3.17.

The most important facility is the time factor. Thirty-three per cent of respondents desire this. Managers of adult education programme should ascertain the convenient timings of both men and women. Classes could be had between the evening and night prayers so far as men are concerned. For women they would like to have classes in the afternoon, between 3 and 5 p.m.

Some of them (14%) desire to have dedicated teachers who could create interest among the people. Separate arrangements for Muslim women are expected by 25% of respondents. It does not mean that Muslim women would not like to mix with Hindu women. What the menfolk say is that women should not mix with men. More emphasis is placed on religious contents as suggested by 18%. If some religious contents are included then there will be additional attraction. This does not mean that general topics should not be there at all. Knowledgeable persons would say that efforts should be made to provide opportunities for integration. But as Muslim society is very sensitive to religion, it would be better to have some contents explaining salient features of the Islamic way of life. There is also a suggestion made by 10% respondents that there should be more emphasis on professional work. This is supported by knowledgeable Muslim in group discussions. Muslims

TABLE 3.17

Facilities Required for Adult Education

Facilities	*Old Mysore Area*		*North Karnataka Area*		*Total*	
	N	%	*N*	%	*N*	%
Convenient timings	140	33.7	102	33.3	242	33.5
Dedicated teachers	58	13.9	40	13.1	98	13.6
Arrangements in Muslim areas for Women	102	24.5	80	26.1	182	25.2
More emphasis on religious Education	70	16.8	58	19.0	128	17.7
More emphasis on professional work	46	11.1	26	8.5	72	10.0
Total	416	100.0	306	100.0	722	100.0

are involved in trades such as agarbathi, beedi, sericulture etc. If the contents have reference to these occupations, giving both merits and demerits, something on health problems likely to arise from some occupations, new technology, then there will be more enthusiasm, Pictorial presentation was also felt necessary.

There is not much difference between the two areas excepting some marginal variations in figures. This would mean that Muslims of both the areas are prepared to participate in adult education programmes if some facilities are provided. Some of the suggestions made by the respondents were endorsed later by the knowledgeable Muslims.

CHAPTER IV

People's Awareness of Programmes

The various Five Year Plans do have quite a lot of programmes for the development of rural people. These programmes are of a general nature and therefore, are not exclusively for Muslim development. Muslims, as a part of the rural society, are entitled to take advantage of these programmes.

But availment of the programmes depends upon or is conditioned by several other related factors. The most basic factor, essential to determine Muslim participation in rural development programmes, is the very awareness of these programmes. If people are aware, then they might have a share in the pattern of utilization. Otherwise, even though the programmes exist, they are of no use to the people. Hence, an attempt was made to find out the awareness of programmes under the Five Year Plans. The information so obtained is presented in a few tables here.

Table 4.1 deals with the general awareness of programmes. As done earlier, this awareness situation is analysed with

TABLE 4.1

Awareness of Programmes under Five Year Plan

Awareness	*Old Mysore Area*		*North Karnataka Area*		*Total*	
	N	%	*N*	%	*N*	%
Fully aware	21	5.0	15	4.9	36	4.9
Mostly aware	29	6.9	19	6.2	48	6.6
Partly aware	65	15.7	42	13.7	107	14.9
Not at all aware	301	72.4	230	75.2	531	73.6
Total	416	100.0	306	100.0	722	100.0

reference to the Old Mysore area and North Karnataka area. It is seen from this table that nearly three-fourth of the respondents (73.6%) are absolutely unaware of the programmes under the Five Year Plans. Even among those who are aware of the programmes, we find different degrees of awareness. The majority of them have only partial knowledge.

The pattern is more or less similar in both the areas. However, respondents of the Old Mysore area are slightly better than the North Karnataka area. But this difference is virtually insignificant.

What comes out of this analysis is that about threefourths of the respondents are not aware of the various programmes under the Five Year Plans. Perhaps this lack of awareness could be a significant reason for the poor participation of Muslims in rural development programmes.

Sources of Awareness

The knowledgeable respondents were asked to comment on the various sources of information. It was found that the Muslim factor played a very insignificant role. While Muslim officers accounted for 10%, the Hindu Officers had an edge over them with 11.5%. Similarly, knowledgeble Hindus were a better source of information than knowledgeable Muslims, the percentages being 10.0 and 8.6. Muslim political leaders accounted for 11.5%, while Hindu political leaders for 13.9%. So far as the role of the organisations is concerned, it was observed that Muslim organisations had absolutely nothing to do with awareness, while the Hindu organizations had something to do, though forming a very small percentage of 4.3.

Lately, Radio, T.V. and literature have become important sources of communication concerning the various programmes of the state. When this issue was discussed with the respondents it was found that literature accounted for about 7% Radio and T.V. for 9%.

There was not much difference between old Mysore and North Karnataka areas. This informaton throws light on the poor sources of information that the Muslim respondents have. What is more distressing is the fact that Muslims, whether Officers or political leaders or organisational workers' have been a very poor source of information. This necessitated further discussions with the Muslims in small groups so that better insights could be obtained.

Muslim respondents were highly critical of Muslim officers. These officers rarely visit the villages dominated by Muslims and discuss developmental programmes. There were instances where special Deputy Commissioners and Assistant Commissioners were Mulims having their Head Quarters within 8 to 10 Km. from the Muslim dominated villages. One could reasonably expect a helpful role from these Officers. But the social situation is highly disappointing. The respondents said that Muslim Officers feel shy and scared of the Muslim beneficiaries. "They are more concerned about their job. They do not want to give the impression that they are communal. They help the Hindus, but not the Muslims". These were the immediate remarks of some Muslims.

The respondents commented on the role of the Muslim political leaders. The reaction was unfavourable. They were of the opinion that a vast majority of the Muslim leaders of various political parties have very little concern for the Muslim cause. They would normally avoid visiting the constituency in general and Muslim segments of the constituency in particular. They did mention names of a few Muslim political leaders who did some positive service to the Muslims. But a vast majority of these leaders would do nothing except make different types of promises during the election period and would not return to the scene immediately after the elections. A general feeling seems to emerge among the Muslims that it will serve no purpose to elect Muslim leaders without a commitment to Muslim development.

So far as knowledgeable Muslims are concerned, the respondents feel that there are a limited numbr of Muslims who have a basic knowledge of the developmental inputs. Even the school teachers have not applied their mind to know what is going on in the State. The religious leaders have a poor knowledge of the programmes for the poor. Similarly, the various Muslim organisations are also unaware of the Governmental programmes. Some of the Muslim respondents reacted sharply by saying "These Muslim religious organisations just tell us to fast for 30 days, offer prayers five times a day and be orthodox Musalmans. But they fail to realise that acute poverty cannot promote religious adherence".

On the other hand, the Hindu factor seems to be more favourable to Muslim development. Persistent questions were put to the Muslim respondents to elaborate and justify their stand. They say that in such villages where Hinds are dominant, Muslims do get some knowledge of the programmes. Secondly, Hindu leaders would depend upon Muslim voters and therefore, they try to do some favours for Muslims, while the Muslim leaders take it for granted that the Muslim vote is always for Muslim candidates.

Awareness of Educational Programmes

There are various schemes of the State to promote educational advancement among people. These schemes are applicable to all sections of society including the Muslims. Some of these programmes are: compulsory primary education, integrated child development scheme, adult education, vocational education, population education, health education etc. Each of these schemes has special significance to the Muslims, both adults and children. Taking advantage of these general schemes depends to a larger extent on awareness.

Table 4.2 reveals that generally execpt for adult education, none of the other schemes listed above are known to a vast majority. Compulsory primary education is known to 20% respondents in general. Even here those who have full awareness account for just 5.8%. Thus the ignorant respondents account for 80%. This is a scheme in action in Karnataka since 1961 when the Compulsory Education Act was enforced.

When the two regions are examined, there is hardly any difference between the Old Mysore and North Karnataka areas. Ignorant Muslims are about 80% in both the areas.

Integrated Child Development Scheme (ICDS)

Integrated Child Development Scheme (ICDS) is another landmark in the social responsibility undertaken by the Government to promote the interests of the child and the mother belonging to weaker sections. Currently, this programme is in operation in selected areas of the State. But its awareness among the Muslims is extremely poor, as low as 89.5% in general. Of the remaining respondents, those who have limited awareness account for twice the number of those who have awareness. The area-wise pattern is also similar.

Adult Education

Adult education is one of the oldest programmes of the State. Its awareness is quite encouraging with as high as 57% respondents having its awareness. Of course, those who have partial awareness are more than those who have full awareness, the percentages being 20.0 and 16.2 respectively. The situation is almost similar in Old Mysore area as well as the North Karnataka. In the former area, there is more awareness (60%) than in the latter region (51%).

Vocational Education

Vocational education is gaining ground in the State with quite a few industrial training schools and polytechniques. Even

TABLE 4.2

Awareness of Educational Programmes

Programmes	*Old Mysore Area*					
	Fully aware		*Partly aware*		*Not aware*	
	N	%	*N*	%	*N*	%
1	2	3	4	5	6	7
Compulsory Primary Education	26	6.2	60	14.4	330	79.4
Integrated Child Development Scheme	16	3.8	20	4.8	380	91.4
Adult Education	86	20.6	164	39.5	166	39.9
Vocational Education	24	5.7	46	11.1	346	83.2
Population Education	60	14.4	100	24.1	256	61.5
Health Education	25	6.2	84	20.2	306	73.6

North Karnataka Area (N=306)						Total(N=722)					
Fully aware		Partly aware		Not aware		Fully aware		Partly aware		Not aware	
N	%	N	%	N	%	N	%	N	%	N	%
8	9	10	11	12	13	14	15	16	17	18	19
16	5.2	40	13.1	250	81.7	42	5.8	100	13.8	580	80.4
10	3.2	30	9.8	266	87.0	26	3.6	50	6.9	646	89.5
58	18.9	98	32.0	150	49.1	144	20.0	262	36.2	316	43.8
16	5.2	24	7.8	266	87.0	40	5.5	70	9.7	612	84.8
40	13.1	70	22.8	196	64.1	100	13.9	170	23.5	452	62.6
14	4.5	60	19.6	232	75.9	40	5.5	144	20.0	538	74.5

Note : Horizontal percentages are provided in all these tables totalling to 100% in each of these divisions.

in the regular school curricula, there is a provision for providing vocational training programmes. But this provision is not uniformly distributed among all schools.

It is observed from the table that as high as 85% respondents in general are ignorant of this programme. As usual, those who have partial awareness account for a higher percentage. There is not much difference between the Old Mysore area and North Karnataka area.

Population Education

One of the non-formal educational programmes is population education. The State has endeavoured to propagate this. Even the voluntary organizations are often involved in this area.

Population educational programmes are better known to the respondents compared to the vocational education. About 37% respondents in general are aware of this as against 63% who are ignorant. Those who have partial knowledge outnumber those who have full knowledge. The position is almost identical in both Old Mysore and North Karnataka areas.

Health Education

Health educational programmes are not known to a vast majority. Nearly three-fourths of the-respondents are ignorant of this vital programme. Those who have full knowledge are nearly one fourth of those who have limited knowledge among the respondents in general. The position is similar in both the areas, though the Old Mysore area is slightly better, relatively speaking.

Awareness of Economic Schemes (Agriculture)

The State has introduced many programmes of assistance to the farmers, particularly the small and marginal farmers to ensure better economic conditions. Some of these programmes are land improvement, minor irrigation, crop insurance, hybrid varieties, subsidy, sericulture, social forestry, bank loans, etc. If fully availed, each of these programmes is expected to promote a break-through in the economic conditions of the farmers. But what is basically required is a certain amount of knowledge about these programmes.

Table 4.3 contains data on the awareness of these programmes. Land improvement schemes are one of the solutions to the problems of small/marginal farmers who cannot afford to have larger areas of land. Often the size of land is not viable But there is no way of getting more land. All that could be done is to improve the existing conditions of the land. But the field situation is that as high as 62% of respondents have no awareness of this programme though in existence for a long time. Of these remaining who are aware of it, it is seen that those who are partly aware of the programme constitute a higher percentage (23.6%) than those who have full knowledge (14.5%).

The situation in both Old Mysore and North Karnataka areas is almost identical. The only difference is that in the Old Mysore area those who are fully aware constitute a slightly higher percentage than their counterparts in North Karnataka area. The position is reverse in the case of those who are partly aware of this in both the areas.

Minor Irrigation

Minor irrigation has been recognised by the planners as one of the most important means of rehabilitation of the weaker sections involved in farming. But the data reveal that nearly 70% of the respondents in general are not aware of this. Again a higher percentage of the people have partial knowledge than full knowledge of this.

The situation in both the areas has only small differences which are not significant in the light of the awareness issue. In

TABLE 4.3

Awareness of Economic Schemes (Agriculture)

Schemas	*Old Mysore Area*					
	Fully aware		*Partly aware*		*Not aware*	
	N	%	*N*	%	*N*	%
1	2	3	4	5	6	7
Land improvement	69	16.6	90	21.6	257	61.8
Minor irrigation	39	9.4	90	21.6	287	69.0
Crop Insurance	25	6.0	65	15.6	326	78.4
Hybrid varieties	89	21.3	160	38.5	167	40.2
Subsidy	89	21.3	160	38.5	167	40.2
Sericulture	99	23.7	107	25.8	210	50.5
Social Forestry	30	7.2	48	11.5	338	81.3
Bank loan	90	21.6	260	62.5	66	15.9

North Karnataka Area (N=306)						Total (N=722)					
Fully aware		Partly aware		Not aware		Fully aware		Partly aware		Not aware	
N	%	N	%	N	%	N	%	N	%	N	%
8	9	10	11	12	13	14	15	16	17	18	19
36	11.7	80	26.2	190	62.1	105	14.5	170	23.6	447	61.9
21	6.8	69	26.6	216	70.6	60	8.3	159	22.0	503	69.7
10	3.2	45	14.7	251	82.1	35	4.8	110	15.2	577	80.0
59	19.2	120	39.3	127	41.5	148	20.5	280	38.8	294	40.7
61	20.0	129	42.1	116	37.9	150	20.8	289	40.0	283	39.2
21	6.8	39	12.8	246	80.4	120	16.6	146	20.2	456	63.2
10	3.2	30	9.8	266	87.0	40	5.5	78	10.8	604	83.7
80	26.1	170	55.6	56	18.3	170	23.5	430	59.6	122	16.9

both the areas, only about 30% of the respondents are aware of this programme, whether fully or partially.

Crop Insurance

Crop insurance has been a long felt need of the farming community. Vagaries of nature would result in crop failure so mush, so that the farmers would have sleepless nights. Later on the State introduced crop-insurance schemes to provide certain amount of stability among the farmers. Taking advantage of this would very much depend upon the knowledge of its existence.

The table provides information on this. In general, 80% of respondents have no knowledge at all. Of the remaining 20% of the people who are aware of this, those who have limited knowledge account for a higher percentage than those who have full knowledge, the percentages being 15.2 and 4.8 almost a 1:4 difference.

Though the position is almost similar in Old Mysore and North Karnataka areas, the former has a slight edge over the later, with a difference of about 4% in its favour.

Hybrid Varieties

Advancement of science and technology in the agricultural sector has brought out significant changes in croping pattern. Traditional crops and technology are being gradually substituted wherever possible. Awareness of this is an important requirement if one has to take advantage.

It is observed from the table that the majority of the respondents in general are aware of the hybrid varieties (59.3%). Among those who are aware of this, more respondents have partial knowledge (38.8%) than those who have full knowledge (20.5%). This is also the position in both the regions.

Subsidy

Subsidy scheme is gradually catching up. About 61% respondents in general are aware of this scheme. Those who have partial knowledge account for twice the number of those who have full knowledge. The situation is almost identical in both the regions, though Old Mysore area has a slight edge.

Sericulture

Sericulture in its various manifestations has made a remarkable advance in Karnataka. Due to the sustained efforts of the Government in general and the then Director of Sericulture[1] in particular, many small and marginal farmers as well as landless labourers have been able to improve their economic status largely because of sericulture. The State has accorded all possible facilities for rearing cocoons, reeling and marketing the products.

However, the question whether the Muslims are also able to take advantage of these facilities is important because at the individual level, there are quite a few silk merchants who have made a name and wealth. But what is the position at the level of a common man ? Is there adequate awareness ? The answer is that awareness of the various facilities has not been spread among all the rural Muslims. In general, awareness is to the extent of 37% only. This is something that goes against the progress of the Muslim masses.

When analysed further, it comes to surface that this overall poor percentage of awareness is due to the situation in the North Karnataka region. Sericulture is well established and has become popular in the Old Mysore area, whereas it is still unknown to many in North Karnataka. In the former region, awareness is to the extent of 50.5%. While it is almost equal

1. Mr. V. Balasubramanian, IAS made a great contribution to the rapid development of sericulture in Karnataka.

between those who are fully aware and partially aware, it is quite different in the North Karnataka area where it is 7% full awareness and 13% partial awareness.

Social Forestry

Social forestry scheme is gaining popularity as it is generally meant to help the weaker sections of the Society. State Government is taking steps to propagate this scheme. But the awareness among Muslims is extremely poor, as high as 84% not being aware of it. Even among those who are aware of, those who have partial knowledge account for twice the number of those who are fully aware of.

Though the situation is almost identical in both the areas, Old Mysore area has a slight edge over the North Karnataka area in terms of awareness, both total and full awareness.

Bank Loans

One of the sober effects of nationalisation of banks is the emergence of social control over banking operations. The result is that today banks have become the major financial source for the poor as against the exploitive traditional money lenders.

Awareness of bank loans is to the extent of 83% in general and around that in both Old Mysore and North Karnataka regions. However, this awareness is not uniform. Those who are partially aware of bank loans account for a very high percentage in both the regions. While 62.5% are partially aware in Old Mysore, it is to the extent of 55.6% in North Karnataka area.

Awareness of Animal Husbandry Schemes

The need for animal husbandry as a major or subsidiary occupation has been recognized in the process of rural develop-dent in general and weaker sections in particular. The State has introduced quite a number of schemes and also increased the coverage of the beneficiaries. To what extent Muslims are aware of these schemes was examined in the study.

Table 4.4 deals with this issue. The important schemes are: dairy farming, poultry farming, sheep rearing, bee-keeping subsidy and bank loans. There is a tremendous awareness of dairy schemes (85.5%), but a vast majority have only partial knowledge (65.7%) in general. The situation is almost identical in both Old Mysore and North Karnataka regions. The percentage of those who are not aware is slightly higher in North Karnataka region.

Poultry Farming

Poultry farming is slowly catching up and lot of importance is given by the State. Hybrid varieties are becoming more and more popular. Both layers and broilers are accepted by the people. But the actual schemes are not known to 56.5% in general. Those who have partial knowledge account for a higher percentage.

When analysed in the context of regional variations, it is observed that more people are not aware of in North Karnataka region (66%) than in Old Mysore area (49.5%). Further, those who have partial knowledge account for twice the number of those who have full knowledge in North Karnataka area than in Old Mysore area where the difference in percentage is very small.

Sheep Rearing

Subject to the availability of fodder in rural area, sheep-rearing is commonly accepted and developed. Government is also encouraging sheep rearing through loans and incentives. Inspite of this, what is observed in the Muslim circle is that awareness of this is very poor. In general, it is observed from the table that 60.7% Muslims are not aware of this, while

TABLE 4.4

Awareness of Economic Schemes (Animal Husbandary)

Schemes	Old Mysore Area (N=416)					
	Fully aware		Partly aware		Not aware	
	N	%	N	%	N	%
1	2	3	4	5	6	7
Dairy farming	86	20.6	274	65.9	56	13.5
Poultry farming	86	20.6	124	29.9	206	49.5
Sheep rearing	76	18.3	104	25.0	236	56.7
Bee keeping	30	7.2	66	15.8	320	97.0
Subsidy	80	19.2	169	40.7	167	40.1
Bank loan	70	16.8	280	67.3	66	15.9

North Karnataka Area (N=306)						*Total(N=722)*					
Fully aware		*Partly aware*		*Not aware*		*Fully aware*		*Partly aware*		*Not aware*	
N	%	*N*	%	*N*	%	*N*	%	*N*	%	*N*	%
8	9	10	11	12	13	14	15	16	17	18	19
50	16.3	200	65.4	56	18.3	136	18.8	474	65.7	112	15.5
34	11.1	70	22.9	202	66.0	120	16.6	194	26.9	408	56.5
34	11.1	70	22.9	202	66.0	110	15.2	174	24.1	438	60.7
10	3.3	22	7.2	274	87.5	40	5.5	88	12.2	594	82.3
30	9.8	100	32.7	176	57.5	110	15.2	269	37.3	343	47.5
26	8.5	184	60.1	96	31.4	96	13.3	464	64.3	162	22.4

those who have partial knowledge account for a higher percentage than those who have full knowledge.

In both Old Mysore and North Karnataka areas also a similar pattern prevails. However, there are more people in North Karnataka area who have no awareness (66%) than in Old Mysore area (56.7%). Similarly, a relatively higher percentage of respondents have full knowledge than in North Karnataka area.

Bee-keeping

Bee-keeping is another activity of some people in rural areas, though not uniformly spread out. Awareness of this programme is very poor among the respondents. Eighty two per cent of respondents in general have no knowledge of this scheme. Among the limited number of those who are aware of this, those who have full knowledge account for a very low percentage. The situation is identical in both the areas. However, in North Karnataka area more people are not aware (89.5%) as compared to the respondents of Old Mysore area (77%). Further, in both the areas those who have full knowledge are not even half of the total number of respondents who have knowledge of this.

Subsidy

Subsidy for animal husbandry programmes is also a well devised scheme of the State. For various reasons people have inhibitions in the beginning to get involved in some of the animal development programmes. Therefore, the State has made available some subsidy schemes.

It is seen from the table that in general the majority of the Muslims are aware of this (52.5%). Those who have partial knowledge account for a little more than twice the number of those who have full knowledge.

Area-wise analysis shows that in North Karnataka region there are more people who do not know the scheme (57.5%) than in Old Mysore area (40.1%). Further, while in the North Karnataka area the number of those who are not aware of this scheme is thrice the number of those who are aware of it, in Old Mysore area the difference is almost half.

Bank Loan

Bank loans are available for animal husbandry schemes. But the awareness of this is extremely poor. Just 22.4% respondents in general are aware of this. Those who have partial knowledge account for 64% as against those who have full knowledge (13%). But when analysed area-wise, it is evident that North Karnataka area, as usual, lags behind. While 31.4% respondents are not aware of this scheme in North Karnataka area when compared to 15.9% in Old Mysore area. Even among those who have awareness, those who have partial knowledge account for a very high percentage in both the areaa. While 16.8% have full knowledge in Old Mysore area, it is 8.5% in North Karnataka area.

Awareness of Economic Schemes (Employment and Wages)

The various Five Year Plans have included schemes for assuring a certain amount of employment and improved wages in the context of rural development. Rural people do suffer from both unemployment and underemployment because of the uncertain conditions of the agricultural operations, besides too much of dependence on it. Hence certain relief programmes have been formulated. Besides this, wage structures suffer both from inadequacy and uncertainty. Legislations have been enacted from time to time. How far have these measures helped the Muslims? This basically depends upon the awareness of the very existence of these measures.

Table 4.5 has information on this awareness. Nearly two-thirds of the Muslims in general are not aware of rural

TABLE 4.5

Awareness of Economic Schemes (Employment and Wages)

Schemes	*Old Mysore Area (N=416)*					
	Fully aware		*Partly aware*		*Not aware*	
	N	%	*N*	%	*N*	%
1	2	3	4	5	6	7
Improved wages	70	16.8	120	28.8	226	54.4
Minimum wages	20	4.8	60	14.4	336	80.8
Equal wages for equal work	4	1.0	11	2.6	408	96.4
Rural employment	62	14.9	100	24.0	254	61.1

North Karnataka Area (N=306)						Total (N=722)					
Fully aware		Partly aware		Not aware		Fully aware		Partly aware		Not aware	
N	%	N	%	N	%	N	%	N	%	N	%
8	9	10	11	12	13	14	15	16	17	18	19
22	7.2	50	16.3	234	76.5	92	12.7	170	23.6	460	63.7
18	5.9	42	13.7	246	80.4	38	5.0	102	14.1	582	80.6
6	1.9	14	4.6	286	93.5	10	1.4	25	3.5	687	95.1
42	13.7	60	19.6	204	66.7	104	14.4	160	22.2	458	63.4

employment schemes (63.4%). Among those who are aware, a higher percentage have only partial knowledge. This is also the situation in both the regions. While a little less than two-thirds are not aware of this in Old Mysore area, this accounts for two-thirds in North Karnataka region. In both the areas, there are more people having partial knowledge than full knowledge.

Improved Wages

There are three issues revolving around wages. These are: improved wages, minimum wages and equal wages for equal work. It is seen from the table that nearly two-thirds in general are not aware of improved wages. Among those who are aware, those who have limited knowledge account for twice the number of those who have full knowledge.

There are significant differences between the Old Mysore area and North Karnataka area. While in the former area a little more than half of the respondents (54.4%) are not aware, it is slightly more than two-thirds in North Karnataka area (76.5%). Among those who have the knowledge of this, we notice that in both the areas those who have partial knowledge constitute about twice the number of those who have full knowledge.

Minimum Wages

The concept of minimum wages is not known to a vast majority (80.6%) in general. Those who have partial knowledge account for nearly thrice the number of those who have full knowledge. This is more or less similar in both Old Mysore and North Karnataka areas.

Equal Wages for Equal Work

Generally, the employers try to exploit the labourers, particularly famale labourers, while giving work and payment of wages. The State has taken cognizance of this and has drawn certain measures. But the awareness is virtually not there. Nearly 5% respondents in general have this awareness. It means 95% are not aware at all. There is an almost identical situation in both Old Mysore and North Karnataka regions.

Awareness of Health Programmes

Health programmes constitute one of the major policies of the State. This is particularly so in the case of the rural poor who often cannot depend upon the private medical practitioners. There are various programmes such as child health, immunization, family planning, dental health, tuberculosis, cancer, AIDS, rehabilitation of handicapped children, etc. Taking advantage of all these programmes depends largely upon the awareness created among the people.

The position of awareness of all these programmes is examined with the help of data presented in table 4.6. Child health programmes are known only to a small number constituting 19% in general. The position is slightly better in the Old Mysore area (20%) than in North Karnataka area (18%). Thus, it means that though the programmes have been in existence for some time, a vast majority of the Muslims do not know this.

Immunization

Children become victims of polio because of the negligence on the part of the parents who fail to get the children immunized. This failure is generally attributed to a lack of awareness and facilities. Nearly 17% of the Muslims in general are aware of this, while 19% are aware in the Old Mysore area, 13% are aware in the North Karnataka area.

Family Planning

Family planning is still a controversial programme among Muslims. Opinion is sharply divided on the main consideration

TABLE 4.6

Awareness of Health Programmes

Programmes	*Old Mysore Area (N=416)*			
	Aware		*Not Aware*	
	N	*%*	*N*	*%*
1	2	3	4	5
Child Health	85	20.4	331	79.6
Immunization	80	19.2	336	80.8
Family Planning	360	86.5	56	13.5
Dental Health	50	12.0	366	88.0
Tuberculosis	80	19.2	336	80.8
Cancer	25	6.0	391	94.0
AIDS	0	—	416	100.0
Rehabilitation of physically handicapped	60	14.4	356	85.6
Rehabilitation of mentally handicapped	40	9.6	376	90.4

North Karnataka Area (N=306)				Total (N=722)			
Aware		*Not Aware*		*Aware*		*Not Aware*	
N	%	N	%	N	%	N	%
6	7	8	9	10	11	12	13
55	18.0	251	82.0	140	19.3	582	80.7
40	13.0	266	87.0	120	16.6	602	83.4
260	85.0	46	15.0	620	85.9	102	14.1
30	9.8	276	90.2	80	11.0	642	89.0
40	13.0	266	87.0	120	16.6	602	83.4
15	4.9	291	95.1	40	5.5	682	94.5
0	—	306	100.0	0	—	722	100.0
30	9.8	276	90.2	90	12.5	632	87.5
21	6.9	285	93.1	61	8.4	661	91.6

whether Islam permits or prohibits. Any way, to what extent are Muslims in general aware of this. A vast majority with 86% are aware. The situation is almost identical in both the areas.

Dental Health

Until recently dental health programmes remained unknown to rural people in general. People were not aware of the importance of dental care. However, the State has undertaken many measures to propagate its importance and involve people in taking advantage of them. But as seen from the table, only 11% Muslims in general are aware of this. Muslims in Old Mysore account for a marginal increase over Muslims in North Karnataka area.

Tuberculosis

Tuberculosis is one of the deadly and dreaded health problems. Though significant efforts have been undertaken all these years, both preventive and curative, its success depends very much upon the awareness among people. It is observed from the table that 83% Muslims in general are not aware of this health programme. There is a higher percentage (87%) in the North Karnataka area than in the Old Mysore area (81%).

Cancer

Cancer is threatening lakhs of people. Its detection itself is full of problems. Though external appearances could be detected and treated with relative success, its appearance inside the body often goes undetected. Quite often the patient would have reached an advanced stage when hopes are generally belied.

The problem of this disease is still worse among the rural people who have neither knowledge nor facilities. It was found that among the Muslim respondents about 94% were not aware of this disease. The position is virtually identical in both Old Mysore and North Karnataka areas.

AIDS

AIDS is still a mystery and its awareness among people cannot be expected. Among the Muslim respondents it was observed that none had any knowledge about it. People could not even tell whether they had heard this very name. This was the position in both the areas.

Rehabilitation of Handicapped Children

There are two categories of handicapped children, namely physically handicapped and mentally handicapped. Often parents do not know why their children suffer from this. Their general explanation is that it is 'fate'. So far as the programmes to rehabilitate the suffering children are concerned, it is observed from the table that vast majority of the Muslims in general are not aware of the programmes for the physically handicapped children (87%). In between the old Mysore area and North Karnataka area, awareness is slightly better in the former (86% as against 90%). Similarly, programmes for rehabilitation of mentally retarded children are not known to 92% Muslims in general. The position is more or less similar in both the areas, though Old Mysore accounts for a slightly higher percentage of awareness when compared to the North Karnataka area.

Awareness of special schemes for the Minorities

Minorities are assured of certain special schemes for socio-economic development, both at the level of the Central Government and the State Government. It is not enough if schemes are just formulated. People for whom these are meant should have access to the inputs. Before the question of access is examined, what is basically required is the awareness of these measures.

Table 4.7 deals with the awareness of these measures. Six measures are listed here. These are :

TABLE 4.7

Awareness of Special Schemes for the Minorities

Reasons	Old Mysore Area (N=416)			
	Aware		Not aware	
	N	%	N	%
1	2	3	4	5
Minority Development Corporation	80	19.2	336	80.8
Minority Commission	190	45.7	226	54.3
Twenty Point Economic Programmes	10	2.4	406	97.6
15 Point programme for the minority	2	0.5	414	99.5
Minority wings of political parties	290	69.7	126	30.3
Wakfs Development Corporation	310	74.5	106	25.5

North Karnataka Area (N=306)				Total (N=722)			
Aware		Not Aware		Aware		Not Aware	
N	%	N	%	N	%	N	%
6	7	8	9	10	11	12	13
60	19.6	246	80.4	140	19.3	582	80.7
125	40.8	181	59.2	313	43.6	407	56.4
5	1.6	301	98.4	15	2.0	707	98.0
1	0.3	305	99.7	3	0.4	719	99.6
189	61.8	117	38.2	479	66.3	243	33.7
200	65.4	106	34.6	510	70.6	212	29.4

(a) Minority Development Corporation ;
(b) Minority Commission ;
(c) 20 point programme for the minorities ;
(d) 15 point economic programme for the minorities ;
(e) Minority wings of the political parties ; and
(f) Wakf Development Corporation.

Minority Development Corporation (MDC)

It was established in Karnataka about 5 years ago with the intention of formulating certain schemes to improve the economic conditions of the poor among the religious minorities. But its awareness is very poor. Nearly 81% of Muslim respondents in general are not aware of this corporation at all. The position is similar in both the areas.

Minority Commission

The Minority Commission in the State was also established about 5 years ago. The main task of the Commission is to assess the status and problems of the minorities in matters relating to language, security, education, economic and others, and submit the report to the State for relevant social action.

Compared to the MDC, awareness of this Corporation is much better. About 44% respondents in general are aware of this. The extent of awareness in both Old Mysore and North Karnataka areas is also more or less identical. However, there is a slightly higher percentage of awareness in Old Mysore area.

20-Point Economic Programmes

This is a general programme introduced by the late Prime Minister, Mrs. Indira Gandhi. These programmes are expected to cover the general population involved in low-income yielding occupations. Muslims are also expected to have their role and share. But what is distressing is that 98% Muslims in general and also in both the areas are not aware of this scheme though in existence for a long time and wide publicity is said to have been given by the State.

Minority Wings of Political Parties

Quite a few political parties with secular approach have set up minority wings or cells within the party organization in order to tackle the special problems of the minorities. The hierarchical structure starts from State level to grassroot level.

So far as awareness is concerned, it is quite significant. About 66% of Muslim respondents in general are aware. In the Old Mysore Area, the percentage of awareness is slightly higher (70%) than in the North Karnataka area (62%).

15-Point Economic Programme

This is a special scheme exclusively meant for the benefit of the minorities. It covers economic, social security, communal harmony, etc. But its awareness is virtually zero in general and in both the areas.

Wakf Development Corporation

This corporation is exclusively for Muslim development and is based on the Wakf property of the community. But the Government has set up a Corporation to monitor the working of the property for the good of the community. A very high percentags of Muslims are aware of this (71%) in general and in both the areas, with Old Mysore having a slightly better edge.

Awareness of Muslim Organisations

There are several organizations started by Muslims to fulfil some of the needs of the community. These organizations are involved in political and non-political activities. Of these, a few were taken up for discussion with the respondents. These are the Muslim League, Baitul Maal, Jamaat-e-Islami, Tabliq-e-Jamaat, Mosque committee and Al-Ameen Trust. People were asked to indicate their awareness and utility of these organizations.

Table 4.8 deals with this awareness issue. In general, a little more than half of the respondents were not aware of the Muslim league (58.6%). This is a political organization of historical importance. It played a significant role during the freedom struggle movement and was ultimately responsible for the creation of Pakistan. Whether there is any need for its continuance after independence and whether its existence has sober or harmful effects on the Muslim mind are not the issues involved in this study. However, whether this organization has been known to people and has any role to play in the socio-economic development of Muslims are the real issues.

But, as pointed out above, its existence is not known to the majority of the respondents. More people do not know in North Karnataka areas (66.9%) than old Mysore areas (52.5%). This variation is perhaps due to the fact that in Old Mysore areas the Muslim League had powerful leaders and it had the wide involvement of supporters, according to some prominent Muslims.

Baitul-Maal is a social organization based on certain principles of Islam. It resembles the Gandhian Trusteeship. Islam has laid down quite a few guidelines for governing the attitudes of the rich towards the poor. Islam has enjoined on the rich their duty to help the needy Muslims. For this purpose, Baitulmaals are established by the Muslims. Collections are made and deposited and used to meet certain minimum requirements of the poor.

But the study reveals that such an important organization is known only to 45.7% Muslims in general. It means the majority

TABLE 4.8

Awareness of Muslim Organizations/Institutions

Organizations	*Old Mysore Area (N=416)*			
	Aware		*Not Aware*	
	N	%	*N*	%
1	2	3	4	5
Muslim League	198	47.5	218	52.5
Baithul-maal	210	50.4	206	49.6
Jamaat-e-Islami	296	71.1	120	28.9
Tabliq-e-Jammat	316	75.9	100	24.1
Mosque Committee	400	96.1	16	3.9
Al-Ameen Trust	310	74.5	106	25.5

North Karnataka Area (N=306)				Total (N=722)			
Aware		Not Aware		Aware		Not Aware	
N	%	N	%	N	%	N	%
6	7	8	9	10	11	12	13
101	33.1	205	66.9	299	41.4	423	58.6
120	39.2	186	60.8	330	45.7	392	54.3
198	64.7	108	35.3	494	68.4	228	31.6
270	88.2	36	11.8	586	81.1	136	18.9
300	98.1	6	1.9	700	96.9	22	3.1
200	65.3	106	34.7	510	70.6	212	29.4

are ignorant. Further, North Karnataka has more Muslims ignorant of this (60.8%) than Old Mysore (49.6%).

This poor knowledge of the very existence of Baitul-maal is a great hindrance to the development of the poor Muslims. And thus the Islamic notion of the duty of the rich towards the poor remains inoperative in actual situations. When further discussed with the knowledgeable Muslim respondents, it was revealed that no efforts are made of late to propagate its importance and people also seem to have lost faith in it as quite a few Baitulmaals have become defunct due to mismanagement and misappropriation of the funds, though collected in the name of religion.

Jamaat-e-Islami

Jamaat-e-Islami is a very powerful and influential Muslim organization generally involved in preparing Muslims for the Islamic way of life. It has been in existence for a long time and has been in the forefront in raising Muslim issues. It conducts workshops and discussion groups methodically and periodically.

So far as its awareness is concerned, the available data presented in the Table indicate that it is widely known to Muslims (68.4%). Its existence is known to more Muslims of Old Mysore (71.1%) than North Karnataka (64.7%). The main reason for this difference in the degree of awareness is due to the fact that the Head Quarters of this organization is located in Bangalore City and has a well organized net work of party activists.

Tabliq-e-Jamaat

Tabliq-e-Jamaat is another well established Muslim religious organisation generally working in small groups. This Jamaat keeps closer social interactions with Muslim men and women separately. The main function of this organization is to propagate religious teachings and make Muslims more and more religious minded.

A vast majority of the respondents are aware of this organization (81.1%). More respondents are aware of this in Northern Karnataka with 88.2% than in the Old Mysore area where the awareness rates 75.9%.

Mosque Committees

In almost all the villages there are mosques. The management rests with the committee generally elected by the Muslims who attend prayers in the Mosque. The mosque committee is in charge of general supervision of the affairs and management of the Mosque. These committees are known to almost all the respondents in both Old Mysore and North Karnataka areas. In fact, these are known to a slightly higher percentage of Muslims of North Karnataka areas than those of the Old Mysore area.

Al-Ameen Trust

Respondents were asked to indicate their awareness of the Al-Ameen Trust for the simple reason that this is a very popular Muslim social organization involved in quite a few educational and banking programmes for the development of Muslims. It has Medical and Engineering Colleges, Polytechnic, Arts and Science Colleges and also Primary schools. It is well known for the Amanath Co-operative Society.

When asked about the awareness of the Trust, a vast majority of the respondents (71%) were able to say that they were aware of it. A slightly higher percentage is seen in the Old Mysore area than the North Karnataka area (74% and 65%).

Awareness of Islamic Principles for Development

The scope of the Islamic message for human development is generally narrowed down to purely religious affairs and often its approach to socio-economic development is lost sight of. This had led to a lack of understanding of its principles or blueprint for development. Islam has many prescriptions for better inter-personal relationships and improved social and economic conditions. To what extent Muslim respondents are aware of this is examined were in brief.

Table 4.9 shows that 63% respondents are not at all aware of the Islamic principles for development. In the Old Mysore area, the percentage of those who are aware of them is 55%, whereas it is much more in North Karnataka (73%).

A further break up of those who are aware of the principles provides further insight into the actual situation. There are three categories of persons—those who are fully aware, mostly aware and partly aware. In general, those who are partly aware constitute 17%. Those who are fully aware form 8% and mostly aware 13%.

Areawise the situation is more favourable in Old Mysore than North Karnataka in all these three categories. Those who are partly aware constitute 19% in Old Mysore, while it is 13% in North Karnataka. Those who are fully aware amount to 9% in the former area and 6% in the latter area.

The next issue that needs further analysis is about the principles. Respondents were asked to comment on what they know. When they were not able to give their answers correctly, some leading questions were put to them. They were asked to comment on hoarding, circulation of wealth, earnings without effort, justification of the means for making wealth, property rights, simple life, interest, profit, education, extravagance, women's status, social participation, freedom, exploitation of labour, black marketing, smuggling goods, corruption, etc.

The issues which were easily understood and commented upon are : interest, profit, education, extravagence and corruption. Other issues were not familiar to most of them. What

TABLE 4.9

Awareness of Islamic Principles for Socio-Economic Development

Area	*Fully aware*		*Mostly aware*		*Partly aware*		*Not at all*		*Total*	
	N	%	*N*	%	*N*	%	*N*	%	*N*	%
Old Mysore	39	9.4	69	16.6	81	19.4	227	54.6	416	100.0
North Karnataka	18	5.9	22	7.2	41	13.4	225	73.5	306	100.0
Total	57	7.9	91	12.6	122	16.9	452	62.6	722	100.0

is most important here is whether in the context of development in general, Islamic principles are relevant. Islam has prescribed, as said earlier, certain guidelines for human progress and development and has stressed that ethics should play a dominant role. But the study indicates that this is not much known to a vast majority of the Muslims.

Social Legislations

The State has introduced many social legislations for the welfare of different sections of society. Though these legislations are not an end in themselves, they definitely constitute an important means through which the socio-economic problems of the suffering groups could be effectively tackled. But for the success of these legislations, what is equally important is the role played by the expected beneficiaries. The basic requirement is the amount of knowledge possessed by them.

The question of awareness of some of the legislations is examined on the basis of the data presented in table 4.10. There are eight social legislations presented here. Each one of them has tremendous influence on the people if they are aware and take advantage of them. How far Muslims are aware of this is an important issue. Normally, Muslims are considered to be quite remote from these issues related to development.

The Minimum Wages Act is virtually unknown to Muslims in general. As high as 91% of them are unaware. Areawise speaking, there is absolutely no difference. In both Old Mysore and North Karnataka areas, the awareness is only around 9%.

Land Reforms Act

The Land Reforms Act of 1961 has undergone both major and minor changes from time to time. It is considered to be a very useful and forceful instrument to ensure a break-through in the socio-economic disparities between the rich land-lords and the tenants. Muslims are both landlords and tenants. They are also expected to possess some knowledge of this law.

TABLE 4.10

Awareness of Social Legislations

Legislations	*Old Mysore Area (N=416)*			
	Aware		*Not aware*	
	N	%	*N*	%
1	2	3	4	5
Minimum Wages Act	40	9.6	376	90.4
Land Reforms Act	190	45.7	226	54.3
Bonded Labour(Abolition) Act	65	15.6	351	84.4
Registration of Births and Deaths Act	15	3.6	401	96.4
Agricultural Income Tax Act	50	12.0	366	88.0
Compulsory Education Act	15	3.6	401	96.4
Special Marriage Act	10	2.4	406	97.6
Muslim Personal Law	35	8.4	381	91.6

North Karnataka Area (N=306)				*Total (N=722)*			
Aware		*Not aware*		*Aware*		*Not aware*	
N	%	*N*	%	*N*	%	*N*	%
6	7	8	9	10	11	12	13
25	8.2	282	91.8	65	9.0	657	91.0
95	31.0	211	69.0	285	39.4	437	60.0
25	8.2	281	91.8	90	12.5	632	87.5
10	3.3	296	96.7	25	3.4	697	96.6
25	8.2	281	91.8	75	10.0	647	89.6
5	2.6	298	97.4	23	3.2	699	96.8
6	2.0	300	98.0	16	2.2	706	97.8
15	4.9	291	95.1	50	6.9	672	93.1

Nearly 40% of the Muslim respondents are aware of this. In fact, this is the highest percentage of awareness among Muslims when their opinion is obtained on other legislations. The Old Mysore area has better awareness then the North Karnataka area. Awareness reaches 46% in Old Mysore area, while it is only 31% in the latter. What is significant here is that Muslims are reasonably aware of this law.

Bonded Labour (Abolition) Act

Bonded Labour is one of the worst social problems being tackled by the State in the rural areas. For the last 10 years attempts have been made to create awareness of the stand of the Government in doing away with this social evil. But the position among Muslims is different. As high as 87% of them do not know. Though in both Old Mysore and North Karnataka regions a vast majority are not aware, the former is slightly better. While 84% of the Muslims of Old Mysore do not know this law, 92% do not know in North Karnataka area.

Registration of Births and Deaths Act

One of the mandatory legal requirements on the part of the parents or the other concerned persons in every family is that whenever a child is born, whether at home or elsewhere, the date of birth should be entered in the Birth Register kept in the Municipality or the Corporation. Similarly, every death case has got to be brought to the notice of the concerned authorities for entry into the records. Registration of both these events has quite a lot of significance. Of late, the State is communicating the importance of this on T.V. Inspite of all this, it is seen that 97% Muslims are totally unaware of this. The position is no better in the two regions of Karnataka.

Agricultural Income Tax Act

This is a piece of legislation to protect the interest of the farmers and as such, rural people in general and Muslims in particular are supposed to be aware of. But it is seen as high as 90% Muslims are not aware of. The situation is equally so in both the areas.

Compulsory Education Act

The Constitution of India provides free and compulsory education for every child in the age group of 6 to 14 years. The State has promulgated the Compulsory Education Act of 1961. Thus, 29 years are over since the Act came into force.

But so far as its awareness is concerned, 97% of the Muslims in general do not know about this. Similarly, in Old Mysore as well as the North Karnataka areas also about 97% Muslims are not aware of this law.

Special Marriage Act

Apart from the personal laws governing marriage, divorce and other related family issues, the State introduced the Special Marriage Act which would enable marriages within the religious group and also between parties belonging to two different religious groups. The main purpose is to promote freedom of choice and give less importance to the traditional religious formalities.

But its awareness is known only to 2% Muslims in general and also area-wise. There is no keenness among Muslims to know this since they are rigidly attached to the Muslim Personal Law.

Muslim Personal Law

Even though Muslims are virtually governed by the Muslim Personal Law, there is hardly any awareness of this. Around 7% Muslims in general know the law. The position is almost identical in both the areas, though Old Mysore area accounts for a little higher percentage of awareness.

Social Security Measures

The concept of 'Welfare State' warrants certain special measures to protect the people against possible risks in life, both relating to person and property. The very goal of the Five Year Plans is to ensure a better standard of living which requires not only inputs for development but also safeguards. There are a number of such measures. Some of them included in the present table 4.11 are : life insurance, health insurance, crop insurance, animal insurance, old age pension, widow's pension, Indira Vikas Patrika, National Savings Certificate, investment in private financial institutions, investment in banks, etc. To what extent are Muslims respondents are aware of these measures ? This question is examined here in brief.

Life Insurance

The Life Insurance scheme has been in existence for the last few decades. In Karnataka, the Government Insurance Department covers all the Government employees as matter of course. Besides this agency, there is the Life Insurance Corporation of India which covers the general public also. But the awareness of Life Insurance is known only to little more than one-fourth of the respondents in general (27%). The situation is almost identical in both the areas, even though a lack of awareness is seen in North Karnataka area.

Health Insurance

Besides the Life insurance scheme, there is also the health insurance scheme which enables people to get medical expenses reimbursed. But its awareness is extremely poor. Only 8% Muslim respondents in general are aware of this. This is also the position in both the areas, with the Old Mysore area having a slightly better edge over the North Karnataka area.

Crop Insurance

From the point of view of the rural people involved in agriculture, crop insurance is a very important scheme. Vagaries in nature affect the prospects of agriculturists. The worst sufferers are the small and marginal farmers. To protect such people the State has introduced the crop Insurance scheme. But

TABLE 4.11

Awareness of Social Security Measures

Measures	*Old Mysore Area* (*N*=*416*)			
	Yes		*No*	
	N	%	*N*	%
1	2	3	4	5
Life Insurance	116	27.9	300	72.1
Health Insurance	40	9.6	376	90.4
Crop Insurance	42	10.1	374	89.9
Animal Insurance	250	60.1	166	39.9
Old age pension	285	68.5	131	31.5
Widow's pension	200	48.1	216	51.9
Indira Vikas Patrika	55	13.2	361	86.8
National Savings Certificate	75	18.0	341	82.0
Investment in financial Private Institution	40	9.6	376	90.4
Investment in Banks	290	69.7	126	30.3

North Karnataka Area(N=306)				Total(N=722)			
Yes		No		Yes		No	
N	%	N	%	N	%	N	%
6	7	8	9	10	11	12	13
76	24.0	230	75.2	192	26.6	530	73.4
20	6.5	286	94.5	60	8.3	622	91.7
28	9.1	278	90.9	70	9.7	652	90.3
39	12.7	267	87.3	289	40.0	433	60.0
85	27.8	221	72.2	370	51.2	352	48.8
75	24.5	231	75.5	275	38.1	447	61.9
35	11.4	271	88.6	90	12.5	632	87.5
35	11.4	271	88.6	110	15.2	612	84.8
21	6.9	285	93.1	61	8.4	661	91.6
210	68.6	96	31.4	500	96.2	222	30.8

Note : Percentage in each case in calculated with reference to the total number of respondents.

this scheme is known to just 10% respondents in general and also in Old Mysore and North Karnataka.

Animal Insurance

Rural people have to depend upon animals like cows, bullocks and sheep for either supplementing their income from agriculture or earning independently. Often these animals beome victims of certain communicable diseases and die. People lose heavy amount. For this reason, animal insurance scheme has been introduced. But the question is whether the rural people are aware of this scheme. It is seen from the table that there is awareness among the Muslim respondents to the extent of 40%. But area wise difference is quite significant. While 60% respondents are aware of this in Old Mysore region, only about 13% are aware in North Karnataka region.

Old Age Pension

Old age pension is another popular social security measure of the State. It has been in existence for some time. Sufficient publicity given to this programme. We find that 51% respondents in general are aware of this. But here also Old Mysore area accounts for a far better status. While 68% are aware in this area, it is only to the extent of 28% in North Karnataka area.

Widow's Pension

This is another popular measure. In general 62% of the respondents are aware of this. But awareness is more among the Muslims of Old Mysore area where it is to the extent of 48%, whereas, it is just half of this in North Karnataka region.

Indira Vikas Patrika

Government of India has introduced Indira Vikas Patrika with the intention of motivating people of different economic levels some part of their earnings for the future. The amount is doubled in about 5 years period. But with all publicity, its awareness is only to the extent of 12% in general among Muslims. In both the areas the position is more or less similar.

National Savings Certificate

National Savings Certificate is more popular among the Government employees as there is some amount of compulsion. But in rural areas the position is not rosy. The table indicates that nearly 85% Muslims in general are not aware of this. More Muslims in North Karnataka area are unaware of this than the Muslims of Old Mysore. While it is to the extent of 82% in the former, it is 89% in North Karnataka area.

Investment in Private Financial Institutions

It is virtually unknown to Muslims. Nearly 92% Muslims in general are not aware. The position is similar in both the areas.

Investments in Banks

Sixty-nine percent Muslims in general are aware of this scheme. In both the areas awareness is known to more or less similar percentage of Muslims.

Discrimination

Social discrimination is against the very spirit of the Indian Constitution. On the other hand, the Govt. have provided special measures to ensure certain amount of equal or equitable distribution of the inputs for development and participation in several forms. This is particularly so in the case of the minorities, besides the Scheduled Castes/Scheduled Tribes.

There is a growing feeling among the Muslims that they are deliberately discriminated against and considered second grade citizens. There are no studies to confirm or reject this feeling. Hence, a few questions were raised in the study to get some feedback from the Muslims. Table 4.12 deals with this.

TABLE 4.12

Sense of Discrimination

Areas of Discrimination	*Old Mysore Area (N=416)*					
	Yes		*No*		*Do not know*	
	N	%	*N*	%	*N*	%
1	2	3	4	5	6	7
Employment in Govt. Service	360	86.5	—	—	56	13.5
Employment in Public Sector	170	40.9	—	—	246	59.1
Employment in Private Sector	210	50.5	—	—	206	49.5
Distribution of Govt. Schemes	370	88.9	—	—	46	11.1
Loan from the Banks	370	88.9	—	—	46	11.1
Tickets for Elections	280	67.3	70	16.8	66	15.9
Representation in Cabinet	190	45.7	—	—	226	54.3
Representation on Boards/Corporations	190	45.7	—	—	226	54.3
Representation on Mandal Panchayats/Zilla Parishads	290	69.7	—	—	126	30.3

North Karnataka Area (N=306)						Total (N=722)					
Yes		No		Do not know		Yes		No		Do not know	
N	%	N	%	N	%	N	%	N	%	N	%
8	9	10	11	12	13	14	15	16	17	18	19
250	81.7	—	—	56	18.3	610	84.5	—	—	112	15.5
120	39.2	—	—	186	60.8	290	40.2	—	—	432	59.8
130	42.5	—	—	176	57.5	340	47.0	—	—	382	53.0
290	94.8	—	—	16	5.2	660	91.4	—	—	62	8.6
280	91.5	—	—	26	8.5	650	90.1	—	—	72	9.9
170	55.6	30	9.8	106	34.6	450	62.3	100	13.9	172	23.8
110	35.9	—	—	196	64.1	300	41.6	—	—	422	58.4
115	37.6	—	—	291	62.4	305	42.2	—	—	417	57.8
185	60.5	—	—	121	39.5	475	65.8	—	—	247	34.2

There are nine areas taken up to examine if discrimination is still practised. These areas were finally selected out of a list containing many more areas. The most important ones as rated by the respondents during the pretesting period are retained. These areas are : Employment in Government service, public sector and private sector; distribution of Government schemes; Loan from the banks, tickets for the elections, representation in the cabinet (council of ministers), representation on boards/corporations, representation on Mandal Panchayats/Zilla Parishads.

Employment : There are three possible sectors where Muslims can try to get in. The most important one is the Government which is the model employer. The State policy is not only to avoid discrimination but also to provide a certain amount of protective discrimination in favour of the minorities who are generally neglected. It is seen that there is none in general to say that there is no discrimination. A vast majority costituting 84% respondents do feel that there is discrimination against the Muslims in Government services, there was no denying, though some are ignorant.

Quite a few associations were able to produce some evidences to prove this point. They argue that if the teachers in Government Urdu schools are excluded for the purpose of calculating the percentage of recruitment, then it hardly comes to about 5.7%. Even this figure is considered to be on the higher side.

Further, even this limited percentage consists of mostly class IV cadre employees. The grouse is that at higher level very poor representation is given. In certain departments like Police, Home Public Works and Revenue, Muslims are openly discriminated against. What Muslim respondents further argue is that even then only those who can grease the palms of the members of the selection committees walk away with the extremely limited jobs. There are quite a few graduates and metriculates without jobs. Whether Government service is worth it or not, people do have the feeling that Government service has security and future.

The position in both the areas remains almost similar and there are no significant differences between them. In group discussions, the rural Muslims in Old Mysore area were more vocal in their complaints against the State than in the North. There are more respondents in the North who have no knowledge of this discriminatory treatment.

Public Sector : The Public Sector presents a different picture. In general, the majority of the respondents, 60% know nothing of the situation. They do not know that there are places in the public sector where they or their children can get jobs, but are discriminated against. Only 40% respondents feel that they are discriminated against.

When the issue was further discussed with the knowledgeable persons in groups, it was evident that their children and relatives had applied for small jobs in some of the industries owned by the State Government as well as Central Government. Many of them were not called for interviews and those who were called for interviews were virtually denied jobs. They are conscious of the fact that the Scheduled Caste candidates are selected. 'We are Muslims and hence not encouraged' is the general feeling among the resopondents.

When pointed out that this could be due to the fact that the non-Muslim candidates are better qualified and experienced, they were thoroughly annoyed and some of them said in a chorus' 'Are we worse than the Harijans?'

There is hardly any difference between the two areas as seen in the table. But in group discussions, people from Old Mysore area were more vociferous and critical. This is perhaps due to their contact and access to some of the major and minor industries in this area.

Private Sector : The majority of the respondents have no knowledge of discrimination in the Private Sector (53%). The remaining 47% do feel that they are discriminated. While the position is identical in the North Karnataka area where it is 57% of respondents not having the knowledge, in Old Mysore area it is 49%. Here 50% know about discrimination. Old Mysore area is slightly better.

The reactions of the respondents are quite interesting. In the first instance, the respondents have no hesitation to say that the private sector is virtually in the hands of the Hindus and as such the Muslims have no right to expect. When asked whether the Government should have a say in the matter and force the employers here to keep certain reservation quota for the Muslims, knowledgeable respondents would just brush aside this question and say 'what sir, how do you expect us to support your argument. When the Government with all the big talk of secularism and equality has almost failed to guarantee jobs to our people in Government offices and Public sector, how can we expect it to order the employers in the private sector to think of us. We should have born as Scheduled Castes'.

Government Schemes : There are a large number of schemes that the Government has introduced for the benefit of the weaker sections and Muslims as a segment of this group do have a right to share. But the study reveals that a vast majority with 91% feel that they are discriminated and denied development inputs. There is none to deny this. Only 9% have no knowledge either way. The situation is slightly worse in Northern area than in Old Mysore area.

Muslim respondents feel that unless they are given certain care and facilities for development, they cannot come up. 'Why should the Government keep us deprived and backward?' Should we not improve our conditions as small/marginal farmers, manual labourers, etc?'

Bank Loan : Banks have to play a big role in the process of transformation of the rural society. They expected to take a pragmatic and helpful stand and see that every deserving individual or group takes maximum advantage and comes up. But the respondents present a different situation. As high as 90% of them are not happy with the banks and are positive and firm in their replies that the banks are not helpful to them in particular. The situation is more or less similar in both the areas.

Respondents do feel that the banks do not have simple procedures. Even non-Muslims also face difficulties in obtianing loans from the bank. It is also admitted that because of misuse of the loans, banks are rigid. But what the Muslims say has a significant point. If they give loans to us and we also fail, then they need not give. But they do not have the mind to help us'.

Tickets : Respondents were asked to offer their comments on the statement 'Muslims are not given their share while tickets are given by the political parties'. While 24% of them expressed their ignorance of this very issue, 14% rejected the statement. But the majority of them endorsed the statement. To them, injustice to Muslims is a reality.

The situation is more or less similar when the two areas are examined. However, there is a significant difference in regard to those who are not aware of this situation. They could neither endorse nor reject the statement. While 35% of Muslims in North Karnataka could not say either way. Muslims from the Old Mysore area constituted not even half of this percentage (61%). Further, those who could say outright that there is discrimination against Muslims were less in North Karnataka than in the Old Mysore area. There is another important difference, namely those who do not agree with this view are more in Old Mysore (17%) than in North Karnataka (10%).

But the mind of the rural Muslims who have some insight into this problem becomes clearer when the results of group discussion are analysed. Muslims have been the traditional vote bank as the Scheduled Castes. They have been supporting the Congress (I). Occasionally, some of them shift their loyalty to other parties too. There are not many Muslims in the Communist parties. So far as the BJP is concerned, Muslims have nothing to do with this party. What Muslims argue is that though they support the Congress party, they are not properly taken care of by the party in many areas of interest. "Sir the party knows our weakness. The leaders know that somehow we vote only for Congress, whether we are benefitted or not. We have been supporting the party under all circumstances. Our political leaders are also not keen on taking up the general case".

The main argument advanced is that their quota is very poor. They should somehow get 30 aeats for the Legislative Assembly, tickets based on their population. But they hardly get 10 to 15 seats. According to them, the Scheduled Castes and Scheduled Tribes get the minimum of about 40 seats at 18% of their population. Vakkaligas and Lingayats get more than their population criterion. In fact, they dominate in the political affairs.

So far as the other parties are concerned, Muslims have a poor opinion. Their reaction was, "When some of us supported the Janata Party some time ago, we had high hopes. But we were disappointed since the treatment was still worse. Our quota was extremely marginal. Hence, we had to shift our loyalty once again in favour of Congress. We had no other option. This is how we are politically exploited and discriminated against".

Representation in Cabinet : Ministry formation is considered a tough exercise since various social groups need to be represented. Muslims, as an imporant minority group, have a special reason for adequate representation in the Council of Ministers. Whether rural Muslims are seized of this issue is an important and interesting point. Hence this aspect was also included in the study.

The data reveal that while there is none in general to deny that the Muslims are discriminated against while ministry is formed, the majority remain ignorant of this. They say that they do not know about ministry formation and the adequacy or inadequacy of Muslim representation. However, 42% respondents who are knowledgeable do feel that Muslims are discriminated against. The situation is similar in both the areas. Of course, there is a higher percentage of those who say that they are ignorant of the issue in North Karnataka area rather in Old Mysore area.

The Muslims' grouse is that they from the major supporters of the Congress (I). Sometimes they support the opposition party also depending upon the circumstances. Even when they have 12 to 15 members in the Legislative Assembly, there will be one Cabinet minister and one State or Deputy Minister. In contrast, they allege that the dominant caste groups will have a lion's share.

Corporations/Boards : Often the State Govenment constitutes various Corporations and Boards for development purposes. Sometimes political needs also play an important role. The question is, what is the share of the Muslims? The respondents feel that they are discriminated against. While no one denies discrimination, the majority are ignorant. But 42% in general do feel that they are let down. In both the areas this is the feeling.

Mandal Panchayats : The State introduced revolutionary measures for transferring power to the people through the Karnataka Zilla Parishad and Mandal Panchayats Acts. The Act provides for reservation in favour of SC/ST and also women.

But there is no reservation for the minorities. In the absence of this facility, it is felt that there is no proper representation to the Muslims. While 66% in general saw that they are discriminated against, 34% are ignorant.

The respondents in both the area express more or less similar views. Those who feel that Muslims are discriminated against, account for a higher percentage in the Old Mysore area (70%), while it is 60% in North Karnataka. But in the latter area, there are more people ignorant of this.

CHAPTER V

Muslim Women in the Context of Rural Development

Women in general have been generally neglected and subjected to socio-economic inequalities. "In both the industrialized advanced and less developed countries women are burdened with cumulative inequalities as a result of socio-cultural and economic discriminatory practices which, until recently, have been take taken for granted as though they were part of the immutable scheme of things established by nature".[1]

Women have a major role to play in the process of rural society. "It has been argued that the Nation's well being as well as that of its women depends upon development policies, programmes and research that fully utilize women's potential"[2]. Women played a notable part in the village household and

1. Alfred D'Souza, Women in Contemporary India, Delhi : Manohar, 1975, P.I.
2. A Seminar Report, "Role of Rural Women in Development" Agricultural Development Council, New York, October 1975.

cottage industries and thus contributed their share to economy in the past. But with the disappearance of such industries in the present times, they have been pushed to the corner where they remain inactive economically and add to the burden of the family.[1]

Apart from the possible role of women in quite a few economic activities, they have a significant role to play in social development too. Some such areas of activities are health, education, recreation, family welfare and so on. Women have inherent capabilities to take up the challenges. Woman power is at times stronger than man power. Man may be physically stronger. But women can subdue the man and force him for development if she can make use of her non-physical strength. She has a big role to play in various social organizations. There are a number of schemes and social legislations to promote the interest of woman.

This is the general view of woman's place in the society particularly so in the Indian Society. But the big question is what is the place of Muslim woman today in the Indian society ? Can a Muslim woman be different from a Hindu or Christian woman ?[2] How does the Muslim religion treat a woman ? How does the Muslim society practice ? In the context of rural development, what role Muslim woman play and can play ?

In the present study, a brief attempt is made to assess the position of Muslim women. Islam has, contrary to popular views among non-Muslim, has accorded a relatively respectable and better status to Muslim woman. She has near equality with man. She has a right to participate in domestic as well as

1. Khan, Mumtaz Ali and Noor Ayesha, Status of Rural Women in India, Delhi, Uppal Publishing House, 1982, P. 3.

2. For a comprehensive general reading of Status of Rural Muslim Women, read Khan Mumtaz Ali and Noor Ayesha, op. cit.

non-domestic activities. She has a right to education. She is not subordinate to man in the strict sense of the term. The Holy Prophet emancipated women in his time and raised their status.

But the present social situation is vastly different. Muslim males have placed innumerable restrictions on Muslim woman's liberty, equality and fraternity. Though all this is unIslamic, not many men and women have protested against the evil practices which have reduced the status of Muslim woman today.

Thus, it becomes quite interesting to attempt a situational analysis of the conditions of Muslim women in the context of various measures of the State for development of rural women in general. As pointed out by Indu Menon,[1] a major index of modernization of any society is the position of its women vis-a-vis men. In a developing society such as India, it is essential that both men and women play equal and important role in the development effort.

The educational and economic conditions of Muslim women as examined in the present study have been explained in the earlier chapters where general conditions of Muslims in rural Karnataka are taken up. In this Chapter, an attempt is made to present certain general issues which are relevant to women's participation in development. These issues are :

1. Opinion about inputs for development;
2. Opinion about training facilities in certain economic activities;
3. Consultation by men with their women folk;
4. Role of women in decision making;

1. Menon, Indu, Status of Muslim Women in India, New Delhi, Uppal Publishing House, 1981, P.I.

5. Opinion about role of Mnslim women in socio-economic development;
6. Awareness of educational programmes;
7. Awareness of social security measures;
8. Awareness of Muslim organization/institutions;
9. Participation in social organizations;
10. Participation in educational programmes;

As pointed out earlier, only a small sample of 120 Muslim women was draw to obtain relevant information on these issues. Data are presented in a few tables.

Inputs for Development

Woman's development question has engaged the attention of those who are seriously concerned about the development of the country. The various plans and programmes remain incomplete unless women are sincerely involved in all the developmental processes. Muslim women are generally kept out of such processes, according to popular notion. It was felt desirable to find out from the rural Muslim women what do they need for development. The opinion is presented in table 5.1.

How many women desire to work on farm to earn their livelihood or supplement the earnings of their menfolk ? Only 25% desire jobs on farms. While 17% cannot give any answer, 58% feel that they do not desire to work on farm. The reason advanced for this is that their cultural conditions do not permit. "Muslim society is different from the Hindu society so far as women's role outside the home is concerned", according to some knowledgeable women. They feel that a woman can and should earn something for the family in these hard days. But they say this should be from some other source.

Those who desire to work on farm say that in the presence of acute poverty and helplessness, there is no option but to earn

TABLE 5.1

Opinion About Inputs for Development

Inputs	*Desire*		*Do not desire*		*Do not know*		*Total*	
	N	%	*N*	%	*N*	%	*N*	%
Jobs on farms	30	25.0	70	58.3	20	16.7	120	100.0
Cottage industries	75	62.5	15	12.5	30	25.0	120	100.0
Loans	69	57.5	31	25.8	20	16.7	120	100.0
Land grant	80	66.7	10	8.3	30	25.0	120	100.0
Improvement of land	80	66.7	10	8.3	30	25.0	120	100.0
Good cows	65	54.2	35	29.2	20	16.6	120	100.0
Sericulture	55	45.8	25	20.8	40	33.4	120	100.0

from any possible way. "It is better to work hard on the farm for the sake of the family rather than attempting to steal or cheat. We do not think Islam has imposed any prohibition as women who need money to lead an honest life. All these restrictions are imposed by our own people". This is how some women reacted in group discussion.

Cottage Industry

In contrast, there is tremendous enthusiasm among women for cottage industries. Sixty two per cent women desire cottage industries. Only 12% do not desire. Of course, 25% women cannot say anything.

Those who desire cottage industries advance quite a few reasons for this. They can take care of family responsibilities. Children can go to schools. Husband's needs can be taken care of. They can work at home during spare time. A sort of dignity is attached to the women who stays at home and earns for the family. This is how women react to the importance of cottage industries.

Wowen who desire cottage industries are ready to take up any industry which has market. They are prepared to learn. All that they want is assured raw materials and market.

Loan

Loan or borrowing is needed for various purposes. Sometimes it would be for productive purposes and sometimes for consumption purposes. Muslim women were asked to comment upon loan. About 57% women were of the view that they would resort to taking loan whenever there is a need. Some of them remarked "How can we, poor people, manage our family affairs without loan ? We need loan for various purposes. Sometimes we need it to carry on our economic activities and sometimes for family maintenance".

But when further probed, they said that taking loan without

a just cause is bad. "If we take loan just because it is available, we take endlessly and face serious consequences when we have to repay". "But loan for improving sericulture, agriculture, dairy, sheep rearing, etc, would help us a lot. We can repay the loan and also make money for further improvement".

There were some women constituting 26% who were not interested in raising loan because of the problem of repayment. Some said 'let us adjust our requirements to the extent of money and capacity we have. Loan is any time dangerous. We lose our name if we do not repay within the due date. Our men-folk become lazy if loan is taken. We do not have peace of mind".

Land Grant

The signifiicance and importance of land is generally known to all the women, whether they have/had land or no land. "Do you want land ?" The answer was 'Yes'. 'Why do you want land ?' Nearly 67% women respondents said that land is an important input for development and therefore, they need it on priority basis. The general reaction was, "if we have land of our own, all of us are tempted to work on it. We cultivate crops and earn more money, we can maintain a few cows. We can do sericulture succesfully. Land gives us status and security".

When asked how much land is required, the answer in general was 'Five acres' of dry land or two acres of wet land'. Women also feel that besides land, they would require inputs and irrigation facilities. Nearly half of these respondents would even suggest theat if a person is hard workind and has moderate quantity of water, he can still earn easily Rs. 600-800 per month on an everage by growing green grass fo cows and mulberry for sericulture.

According to 67% women respondents, improvement of land would ensure adequate returns. They feel that the existing wells and tanks need to be deepened to ensure regular supply of water.

Good Cows

Many women are familiar with rearing of cows. On an average, each family has one cow, but of ordinary quality. A little more than 54% women desire good quality cows. Though they could not give the exact name of such cows, they could convey what they wanted to. Those who did not want good cows form 29%. They do not want because of their inability to take care of these costly cows. Maintenance would be a big problem, according to them, particularly when the cows are pregnant.

Sericulture

In many of the villages, particularly in Bangalore district, women expressed their desire to have facilities for sericulture. These women constituted 46%. Thirty three per cent did not have the knowledge of sericulture at all. These are from North Karnataka. Twenty one per cent did not desire sericulture. It is not because of their lack of faith in this. It was mainly because of non-availability of some facilities including healthy rearing facilities.

Desire for Training

Human resource develoment has gained momentum and significance. Every human being has some potentialities which need to be identified and promoted. Even illiterate people could also be made productive citizens. Women in general and Muslim women in particular are no exceptions. They need training in various areas of social and economic activities so that they could become resourceful persons in the process of development of the family, community and the society.

Based on the current trends, Muslim women respondents were approached to find out their desire for training in a few areas like adult education, cottage industries, dairy and sericulture. Their opinion is furnished in table 5.2.

Adult education has been in existence for a few decades and of late the State policy is very much firm and positive to involve more and more women in non-formal education. As pointed out else where in the present chapter, Muslim women have very little participation for various reasons. But what we now gather from the data presented in the table is that they are not totally averse to receive training in adult education. Fifty per cent women desire this. While 33% do not have any desire, 16.7% remain neutral.

Cottage industries are being encouraged by the State both under the Khadi and Village Industries Board and the general programmes of the State. It is often said cottage industries would suit women in general and backward women like Muslim women who do not generally desire to go outside the family environment for work. When asked about their opinion, 62.5% women said that they would desire to get trained. Of course, the majority of them feel that they would be in a position to take advantage of the training programmes if confined to their own areas and are exclusively for women. Those who do not have any desire for thie training and those who remain neutral constitute 25% and 12.5% respectively.

Dairy industry is catching up among Muslims too. Women have a significant role to play at home in taking care of the animals. They are not generally exposed to new approaches. Dairy technology has undergone lot of improvement. Fifty per cent Muslim women are ready for training. They prefer training in their own or nearby villages. But they are not totally averse to training in distant places if they could get back in the evenings and their menfolk would agree. However, nearly one-third of them are not willing to get trained as it affects family life.

TABLE 5.2

Trainning Facilities

Training	*Desire*		*Do not Desire*		*Donot know*		*Total*	
	N	%	*N*	%	*N*	%	*N*	%
Adult education	60	50.0	40	33.3	20	16.7	120	100.0
Cottage industry	75	62.5	30	25.0	15	12.5	120	100.0
Dairy	60	50.0	39	32.5	21	17.5	120	100.0
Sericulture	51	42.5	30	25.0	39	32.5	120	100.0

Sericulture has made deep impact on the Muslims in certain pockets of the State. Women are playing a significant role. But they are not trained. Quite a few defects are noticed in the process of rearing cocoons and growing mulberry. There is a need for better understanding. But the opinion of Muslim women is not uniform. It depends upon the areas where sericulture has already made a mark. In the present case, 42.5% women desire training and the rest are either not willing or remain neutral.

Social Participation

Social participation could be at two levels, namely family level and community level. Family level includes consultation between the males and females, generally meaning husbands and wives. Community level means participation in formal and non-formal organizations.

Consultation

In a family situation consultation between husband and wife is a healthy sign of adjustments and progress. This type of social interaction is encouraged in Islam. Wife has to be consulted by the husband wherever this is needed. This is examined in the present study. The data are presented in Table 5.3.

In economic matters, 84% women say that they are not at all consulted. Only 17% are consulted some times. In educational matters, the situation is slightly better. While 50% say that they are not at all consulted, among the remaining, some are always consulted (21%) and others sometimes consulted (29%). In matters relating to cultural affairs also 50% say that they are not at all consulted. While 17% say that they are always consulted, 33% say that they are sometimes consulted.

However, in religious matters and marriage affairs, a vast majority say that they are consulted. While 83% say that they are consulted in all matters relating to religious practices and

TABLE 5.3

Consultation with Women

Areas	*Always consulted*		*Sometimes consulted*		*Not at all consulted*		*Total*	
	N	%	*N*	%	*N*	%	*N*	%
Economic matters	—	—	20	16.7	100	83.7	120	100.0
Educational matters	25	20.8	35	29.2	60	50.0	120	100.0
Religious matters	40	33.3	60	50.0	20	16.7	120	100.0
Cultural matters	20	16.7	40	33.3	60	50.0	120	100.0
Marriage alliance	40	33.3	50	41.7	30	25.0	120	100.0

rituals, those who say that they are sometimes consulted from the majority with 50%. Only 33% say that they are always consulted. This is more or less the situation in marriage affairs also. The majority say that they are consulted. Those who are some times consulted account for a higher percentage than those who are always consulted, the percentages being 42 and 33 respectively.

Decision-Making

Islam has provided the best possible status to women. A women has equal rights and opportunities subject to certain restrictions based on health ground. A husband is not considered as the boss of the wife who has to submit herself to the whims and fancies of the husband. It is true that the ultimate authority rests with the husband in the event of an uncompromising situation where it is feared that otherwise the wife will be a potential danger.

In family matters, husband and wife are equal partners with specific responsibilities and division of labour. To what extent the spirit of Islam is noticed in action in Muslim Society. This issue was discussed in brief with Muslim women. The data are presented in Table 5.4.

There are five areas of activities included in table for this purpose. Economic matters, educational matters, religious matters, cultural matters and marriage alliances. It is expected that in all these routine matters of much significance to the family, both husband and wife have equal role in decision making. Further, the role of women in decision making is examined with reference to the extent of effectiveness.

In economic matters, a vast majority of the women respondents (83%) say that their role is not at all effective. Those who say partly effective account for only 17%. None of the respondents say that their role is effective. Even in educational matters the situation is identical. Women has no effective role

TABLE 5.4

Role of Women in Decision-Making

Areas	Fully effective		Partly effective		Not at all effective		Total	
	N	%	N	%	N	%	N	%
Economic matters	—	—	20	16.7	100	83.3	120	100.0
Educational matters	—	—	20	16.7	100	83.3	120	100.0
Religious matters	30	25.0	50	41.7	40	33.3	120	100.0
Religious matters	20	16.6	50	41.7	50	41.7	120	100.0
Marriage alliances	40	33.3	60	50.0	20	16.7	120	100.0

in educating the child. What is further gathered here is that even in matters of routine importance, woman is totally neglected. A husband takes it for granted that the wife is unfit for any advice or suggestion. It is true that the wives are mostly illiterates. But what these women say is that even their husbends are also mostly illiterates. Some women remarked in a group discussion, 'Sir, it is true that most of us are not educated. But there are some issues which do not require educational advantage for us to offer some suggestions. Our husbands think we are all useless creatures. We feel bad, but are helpless because men are dominant'.

The situation is different in matters relating to religion, culture and marriage. It is seen that the majority of the women have a role to play in decision making. In religious matters, 67% say so. But the majority are only partly effective. Women say that they are better suited for religious matters. "It is we who take all the steps to celebrate religious festivals and rituals. Men do not come in the way in all these matters". Even in cultural matters, women have an effective role to play. Only 42% women say that their role is not effective.

The best role played by women in decision making relates to marriage alliances. Only 17% say that their role is not at all effective, while 83% have a role to play. It means in matters relating to marriage, women have a better role while taking decisions.

Social Organizations

Women's participation in social organizations is a great boon to their development. Social organization is both a condition and a process.[1] Participation of women in social situation is their inherent right or privilege. Social organization, if well planned and managed, can be made effective instruments of

1. J.O. Hertzler, Social Institutions, Lincoln : University of Nebraska Press, 1946, P.B,

change in the attitudes and values of rural women. These organizations are both formal and non-formal. The latter has powerful and real influences on the behaviour of people as pointed out by Theodore[1].

Rural societies in under-developed countries or developing countries do suffer not only from the absence of both or either of these two organizations but also from the role of the vested interest have commitment generally to the cause of equal distribution of gains or 'growth with social justice'. The situation is likely to be still worse in the case of rural women in general and disadvantaged women like Muslim women in particular.

It is in this context that a reference to the participation of Muslim women in rural social organizations becomes very relevant and significant.

The various formal and non-formal social organizations in which the rural women are generally expected to participate are :

1. Mahila Mandals,
2. Banks,
3. Primary Health Centres,
4, Village Panchayats,
5. Co-operative Societies, and
6. Educational Institutions.

The question now is whether Muslim women participate in these organizations and if so, to what extent ? A vast majority of Muslim women are aware of these formal and non-formal organizations. They also feel that they may be useful. But their participation is almost negative. Only in two villages, a few Muslim women had become members of the Mahila

1. Theodore T. Herbert, Dimensions of Organizational Behaviour, New York : McMillan Publishing Co. Inc. 1976, P. 297.

Mandals. What prompted them to become members is the pressure of some Hindu women known to them. In all villages where Muslims were either 100% or in majority, there was no Muslim women in any Mahila Mandal. In fact, the concept of Mahila Mandals was totally alien to them. It is only in a few Hindu dominated villages that Mahila Mandals were known to Muslim women also.

When asked as to why either they were ignorant or not participating in Mahila Mandals, women said that their menfolk would not encourage them. These women were confined to their homes. It was only in the case of Tableeq-e-Jamaat that some Muslim women were found active. This is because of religious considerations. Even men would say that there was no need for women's organizations. If men are active and progressive, women's problems could be taken care of.

Banks

A vast majority of women knew the existence of banks and were familar with the transactions carried on by their menfolk. But they were not active members of the banking transaction. A vast majority of women had not opened bank account. The feeling was that there was no need for woman to have their own account in the banks. "When our menfolk are there, why should we bother about separate account in our names?" was the general reaction of women.

Primary Health Centres (PHC)

Muslim women were generally not familiar with Primary Health Centres. Their participation was also minimum. Health care is generally neglected by Muslim women. If they fall sick they would go to nearby town for check up and treatment. As said earlier, it was only in the Hindu dominated villages that Muslim women had some thing to do with the PHC.

1. The explanation given here is based on the group discussions with women respondents.

Village Panchayats

The recent changes in the Panchayatiraj system in Karnataka has created wide awareness among Muslim women also. A vast majority of them participate in the elections. There were 16 Muslim women elected as members of the Mandal Panchayats.

But effective participation was not found any where. They were also irregular to the meeting. In some cases their husbands participated in the meeting. This type of proxyattendance is widely known and tolerated.

Co-operative Societies

Muslim women are generally not familiar with co-operative societies of any type. There was absolutely no society in any of the villages with 100%. Muslim population or even majority Muslim population. In Hindu dominated villages, there were co-operative societies, mostly consumer societies. Muslim women of these villages had known such societies. But they had no participation at all.

Educational Institutions

Wherever Urdu schools existed, there were Muslim women teachers. There were on restrictions on them. But so far as School Betterment Committees are concerned, there were no women members at all. All the members were males. But woman head mistresses attended the meetings whenever called for.

So far as non-formal organizations are concerned, there was absolutely no Muslim woman who had any thing to do with them. Muslim women had nothing to do with religious institutions. Muslim women would not enter the mosques nor was any woman on the Mosque Committees.

Muslim women had nothing to do with village shandies. Only Hindu women had active participation in such shandies.

There were not many recreational organizations in the villages surveyed. But there weie no Muslim women participating in these activities. They had no role to play in the village festival organizations. Reading rooms were virtually unknown to them even wherever they existed.

Role of Muslim Women in Development

It is often said that one of the reasons for the slow progress of Muslims in socio-economic development is the almost total absence of the role of Muslim women in these activities. Men-folk do not permit or encourage them to play their role. But do women really desire to play their role? This question was addressed to the selected Muslim women respondents. The opinion gathered is presented in table 5.5.

Should Muslim women play an effective role? To this question, only 21% women respondents agree while 29% remain silent, 50% do not agree. However, 58%women agree that women should play a moderate role. Moderate role, according to them, would mean such functions which are simple but helpful for improving the socio-economic conditions. They also say that all this depends upon their abilities. Those who could not answer this question constitute 42%.

What is most important in this situational analysis is their response to the question 'Should not women play any role at all in development ? A vast majority of women constituting 83% are against this question. They do not agree that they should not have any role to play.

Further, none of them supported this argument. Only 17% women remained neutral as they could not understand and answer this question.

In several group discussions, what surfaced is the fact that women do have the realization that they should not be passive partners in life. They should be involved in such matters which are directly related to family development. They are

TABLE 5.5

Opinion about Role of Muslim Women in Socio-Economic Development

Opinion	*Agree*		*Do not agree*		*Do not know*		*Total*	
	N	%	*N*	%	*N*	%	*N*	%
Women should play an effective role	25	20.8	60	50.0	35	29.2	120	100
Women should play a moderate role	70	58.3	—	—	50	41.7	120	100
Women should not play any role	—	—	100	83.3	20	16.7	120	100

prepared to do hard work and earn some money which could be supplemented to the earnings of their menfolk.

Awareness of Educational Programmes

Awareness of some of the educational programmes is an important pre-requisite in the process of development of rural women. The position of Muslim women is discussed in brief with the help of data presented in the table 5.6.

Compulsory education which is guaranteed in the Constitution of India and also in the concerned legislation in the State is not known to 75% women. Even among those who have awareness, those who have partial awareness account for twice the number of those who have full awareness.

Integrated Child Development Scheme is another important scheme of the State. But only 25% have this awareness. Even here, those who have partial awareness constitute a higher percentage than those who have full awareness.

There are two programmes which are known to a vast majority. There are adult education and family planning. However, it is noted that even here those who have full awareness constitute a much lower percentage than those who have partial awareness.

Those who have awareness of vocational education, population education and Health education constitute a small percentage only. A vast majority of women have no awareness at all. This is the position of Muslim women inspite of efforts put in by the State for the last several years.

Awareness of Social Security Measures

The various social security measures of the State are expected to be known to men as well as women as both have a right to take advantage of the schemes. This question of awareness was taken up in the present study. The nine schemes

TABLE 5.6

Awareness of Educational Programmes

Programmes	*Fully aware*		*Partly aware*		*Not aware*	
	N	%	*N*	%	*N*	%
Compulsory primary education	10	8.3	20	16.6	90	75.1
Integrated child development scheme	13	10.8	17	14.2	90	75.0
Adult education	20	16.6	65	54.2	35	29.2
Vocational education	—	—	15	12.5	105	87.5
Population education	10	8.3	15	12.5	95	79.2
Family planning	40	33.3	60	50.0	20	16.4
Health education	5	4.2	35	29.2	80	66.6

included in the table 5.7 are : Life Insurance, Health Insurance Crop Insurance, Animal Insurance, Old age pension, Widow's pension, Indira Vikas Patrika, National Savings Certificate and Investment in banks.

The position of awareness of these schemes is mostly unknown to Muslim women. Life Insurance scheme is known to 25% only inspite of the scheme being in existence for a long time and wide publicity. Even among those who know this scheme, only 8% know fully and the rest have only partial knowledge. Health insurance scheme is unknown to 92% women, only 8% have partial informations.

Crop Insurance is an important measure to protect the interest of the farmers. This scheme is virtually unknown to Muslim women. Only 8% women have partial awareness. The position is similar even in the case of animal insurance. Though quite a few families have maintained cows, women are not aware of the very insurance of animals.

But the situation is different in the case of old age pension and widow's pens'on. Two-thirds of women respondents are aware of old age pension. However, those who have partial knowledge account for 54% while those who have full knowledge are to the extent of 12% only. Widow's pension scheme is known to 75% women. But those who have partial knowledge out number those who have full knowledge.

Savings schemes are almost unknown to women. While none of them know National Savings Certificate Scheme, 92% do not know Indira Vikas Patrika as well as investment in banks.

Awareness of Muslim Organizations/Institutions

Awareness of some of the Muslim organizations/Institutions among women is also an important factor in the process of development. But it is often said women have no knowledge

TABLE 5.7

Awareness of Social Security Measures

Measures	*Fully aware*		*Partly aware*		*Not aware*	
	N	*%*	*N*	*%*	*N*	*%*
Life Insurance	10	8.3	20	16.7	90	75.0
Health Insurance	—		10	8.3	110	91.7
Crop Insurance	—		5	4.2	115	95.8
Animal Insurance	—		10	8.3	110	91.5
Old age pension	15	12.5	65	54.2	40	33.3
Widow pension	15	12.5	75	62.5	30	25.0
Indira Vikas Patrika	—		10	8.3	110	91.7
National Savings Certificate	—				120	100.0
Investment in banks	—		10	8.3	110	91.7

of such organizations. Since there are no hard data available on this issue, an attempt was made to examine and analyse the situation. The relevant data are presented in table 5.8.

There are five organizations included here. These are: Muslim League, Baithul Maal, Jamaat-e-Islami, Tabliqu-e-Jamaat and Mosque Committee. It is observed that a vast majority of women are not at all aware of these organizations. Muslim league, a political organization, is not known to 86% women. Baithul Maal, a socio-religious institution for the upliftment of the poor, is also not known to 87% women. Jamaat-e-Islami which is concerned with spreading Islamic way of life through active participation in many public issues is not known to 71%. But Tabliq-e-Jamaat is much better. It is known to 40% women. Normally the organizers of Tabliq-e-Jamaat are interested in women's meeting for propagation of true spirit of Islam. This is done through their women workers.

But what is surprising is that even in the case of mosque committees, only 43% are aware of. Mosque committees exist in all the villages where mosques are located. Mosque committees play an important role in day to day affairs. But women are perhaps not kept informed of all this by their menfolk.

Awareness of Women's Organizations

In none of the villages any Muslim women's organization was found. But in a few villages Mahila Mandals existed. But Muslim women had absolutely no knowledge of these Mahila mandals. An attempt was made to get the opinion of the organizers of the Mahila mandals about non-participation of Muslim women. An almost maximum opinion was that Muslim women are least interested to know that happens outside their homes.

This issue was further raised with Muslim women.[1] They

1. The information furnished here is based on informal group discussions held with women respondents.

TABLE 5.8

Awareness of Muslims Organisations/Institutions

Organization	*Aware*		*Not aware*		*Total*	
	N	%	*N*	%	*N*	%
Muslim League	17	14.2	103	85.8	120	100.0
Baithul Maal	15	12.5	105	87.5	120	100.0
Jamaat-e-Islami	35	29.2	85	70.8	120	100.0
Tablique Jamaat	48	40.0	72	60.0	120	100.0
Mosque Committee	52	43.3	68	56.7	120	100.0

are bounded by their traditional culture that a Muslim women should not have participation outside the family. When asked whether Islam had imposed such a restriction, 90% women expressed their ignorance. All that they could say is that their men-folk would not permit them to have any participation in social organization. But these men have no hesitation to permit their women to participate in Muslim religious organizations like Tableeq-e-Jamaat. The fear expressed is that women should not have any participation in associations where men are likely to have their presence. Further, Muslim women say that their men-folk would insist that Muslim women should maintain their separate identity.

However, in such villages where Muslims are in majority or which are totally Muslim dominant, there seems to be some relaxation in the attitude of Muslim men. They have no objection to their women having meetings among themselves.

To the question whether women's organization exist outside their villages or in towns and cities. Muslim women respondents said that they did not know anything about this excepting the existence of Tableeq groups which were interested in propagating the spirit of Islam. Small group meetings are held by the Jamaat and women feel quite satisfied. When asked whether these meetings help them in any way in tackling day to day socio-economic problems, 75% of them said emphatically 'No'. But the remaining felt that such religious groups do have profound influence on the mind of women who could think of development as contemplated in Islamic literature.

Family Planning

One of the major hindrances of economic development of any group is said to be the large size of the family. Where resources are marginal and dependents are many, dismal economic conditions affect the present as well as the future of the family. The popular view is that Muslims are totally opposed to family planning on religious grounds.

This issue was discussed with women respondents with the help of female investigators in particular. A vast majority of women were not opposed to family planning. They do realize that they could lead a happy life and ensure better future for their children only when they have limited number of children. About 35% women were practising family planning methods. This was possible because of the co-operation of their husbands and lack of opposition to it. But in other cases, a vast majority of women, percentage being around 60, could not adopt because of three important reasons :

1. Islam would not permit killing of the child in the womb.
2. Family Planning methods would lead to to immoral conduct, and
3. Health would be affected.

Since these women could only give the reasons and could not offer clear explanation, it was found desirable to discuss the issue with a relatively more knowledge and open minded women. It is true that killing of an infant in the womb is a sin. This happens only when the women conceives. It is also said that during the first three months the child in the womb is only a lump of flesh and has no life. In such a situation, killing question does not arise at all.

But the other view is that if attempts are made to avoid conception, the question of killing does not arise. About 70% of the women contacted in this regard would agree with this view. In other words, they would not accept the contention that Islam has imposed a total ban.

The second reason that some of the family planning methods might lead to immoral conduct gets support from a vast majority of women. But even then, they give alternative suggestion to overcome this problem. Their suggestion is that unmarried boys and girls should be made to realise that such attempts would be viewed seriously as sins by God. The fear of God alone could prevent the youngsters from abuses. The methods are for a limited and definite use, not for misuse.

The third reason that health gets affected after operations or taking pills seems to be a genuine concern of the people. They quote quite a few instances where women were physically wrecked after using these methods. Whether what they said is true or false, what is significant is that no efforts have been made to convince women that health need not necessarily be impaired because of using the methods. What the family planning workers or doctors tell outside to others would not meet the demand. They should convince women that there is no negative relationship between the adoption and health.

Any way, what seems to be of much importance here is that Muslims women are not opposed to the norm of small size family. They are very much aware of the fact that smaller the size of the family, better would be the family conditions.

Opinion About Education

Women's opinion about education is more important than opinion of men because woman has a better role and ability for providing education at different levels and for different categories of persons. In Table 5.9 the views of Muslim women are examined in areas relating to adult education and education for children, both sexes included.

Seventy five per cent women desire education for male adults. Only 17% say not desirable and the remaining are neutral. So far as adult education for females is concerned, only 25% women respondents desire, while 58% remain neutral. It means that women are either not in favour of adult

TABLE 5.9

Opinion About Education

Types of education	*Desirable*		*Undesirable*		*Neutral*		*Total*	
	N	%	*N*	%	*N*	%	*N*	%
Adult education for males	90	75.0	20	17.0	10	8.0	120	100.0
Adult education for females	30	25.0	20	17.0	70	58.0	120	100.0
Primary education for boys	100	83.3	—	—	20	16.7	120	100.0
Primary education for girls	90	75.0	—	—	30	25.0	120	100.0
High school education for boys	90	75.0	—	—	30	25.0	120	100.0
High school education for girls	20	16.7	80	66.7	20	16.6	120	100.0
College education for boys	50	41.7	60	50.0	10	8.3	120	100.0
College education for girls	10	8.3	90	75.0	20	16.7	120	100.0

education to women or they are not properly motivated to take it up.

In a group discussion, the issue was further probed. Women seem to have some genuine difficulties. They said that domestic works, timings, places and contents of non-formal education poses practical problems. They feel adult women have better and more complex role at home and outside the home and therefore there is no need to bother adult women about non-formal education, particularly in relation to literacy.

So far as education for children is concerned, women are generally in favour. Upto Primary level, women favour education for both boys and girls, the percentage being as high as 75. There is none to oppose. So far as high school level is concerned, while 75% women desire it for boys, only 16.7 desire it for girls. In fact, 66.7% feel that high school education is not desirable to girls. College education is desired for boys to the extent of 41.7% and only 8.3% for girls.

When asked why the majority do not desire high school education for girls, the respondents said 'What is the use of our girls studying upto high school. They do not go for jobs. We may find it difficult to educate boys with our limited income. It is enough if our girls study upto primary level. College education is also not favoured by the majority because to put in the words of the respondents, "Our educated boys remain unemployed. They do not get Government jobs and they do not retain interest in agriculture or dairy. They create problems to us. Why should we give college education to girls ? We do more harm than good to the girls by sending them to college".

Opinion About Employment of Women[1]

Muslim women have realized that they cannot afford to remain idling their time at home after the routine domestic

1. This information was collected in group discussion with selected women respondents.

works are over. A vast majority of them would like to do some economic activity at home and earn a little. They are not keen on being major partners in running the family. They would only supplement the earnings of their husbands. They are of the opinion that self-employment is more desirable than being employed for wages. However, they are not against employment for wages provided they are not made to go a long way.

Child Labour

A vast majority of the women respondents feel that child labour is bad and they would not like to encourage. But there are a few factors which force them to send their children for work. When children refuse to go to school, it is better to see they are employed. Otherwise child would go wrong, according to these women. They, however, say that female children should not be sent out of home for employment. They feel that such employment is bad for the girls.

CHAPTER VI

A Comparative Analysis of the Status of Muslims

There are two broad groups of India Citizens, namely the Hindus and the religious minorities. While the former account for about 80%, the latter have 20% of India's total population. India is a multi-structured society where religious pluralism is recognized and practised. The Constitution of the Country has guaranteed equality of law for all the citizens. However, in the light of certain social realities, Minorities have been granted certain special rights.

Among the various minority groups, Muslims happen to be the largest minority group with 12% population. The next minority group consists of the Christians with 4%. The balance is shared by the Buddhists, Jains and the Sikhs.

Among the Hindus, there are a large number of groups based on the caste system. These groups can be categorised into :

1. The ritually pure and academically advanced Brahmins

2. The economically advanced and dominant non-Brahmin upper castes
3. The socially and economically disadvantaged lower castes consisting of the Scheduled Castes and Backward Castes, and
4. The culturally, socially and economically disadvantaged groups called Tribes.

Among the minorities, the Muslims happen to be the worst group from all counts. Among the Hindus, the Scheduled Castes and the Backward Castes happened to be the worst. In order to uphold the dignity and status of the poor citizens, the State has introduced many special schemes. While the minorities have been granted special safeguards and protection to maintain their minority character and religious freedom and the right to establish and manage educational institutions, the Backward Castes and Scheduled Castes (also S. Tribes) have been granted special protection for educational and social advancements.

While the Muslims have to be contented with religious institutions and educational institutions, the Backward social groups like the Scheduled Caste can march ahead of the Muslims in all fields of developments. In such a situations, it is of great importance and significance to study the relative socio-economic status of the Muslims and the Backward Castes. It is for this purpose that the present study has included a reference to comparative status.

There are a number of Backward Castes in the rural areas, besides the Scheduled Castes. Some of them had absolutely no status in the past. They were a totally neglected lot. In those days, about four decades ago, Muslims had better status and their advancement was quite superior in both social as well as economic fields, apart from religion when compared to the Backward Castes and Scheduled Castes. Where are they today in the context of intervention of the State with the launching of the Five Year Plans for rural development. The normal expectation could be that the status of Muslims is better than either of the two Hindu Backward groups. To test this, the Kumbaras, Kurubas and Tigalas, besides the Scheduled Castes were included in the study. Details of the sampling design are indicated in the Introducing Chapter.

This comparative analysis is made with the help of some statistical data presented in a few group discussions and Case-studies. As said earlier, a comprehensive examination was not possible for want of time and funds. Besides this, the only purpose of the study is to present the situational analysis with reference to the rural Muslims. A small effort is made to provide a comparative status.

The variables included in the comparative study are : occupation, income, land holdings, employment status, awareness of social legislations, economic schemes, social security measures, health programmes, educational programmes and educational status etc. Each of these variables is discussed here with the help of data presented in the tables.

Employment Status

So far as employment status is concerned, there is not much difference between the Muslims and the others excepting some marginal differences as seen in table 6.1. Muslims and the Scheduled Castes are almost on par, about two-thirds being employed. However, there is some difference in the case of the Backwaad Castes who account for 81% employment, 8% more than the Muslims.

The situation would mean that unemployment is not at all problem among all these groups. But when further probed into, Muslims feel that they are discriminated in public sector. They have to heavily depend upon the land and other local sources. Education has no relevance to their employment

TABLE 6.1

Employment Status of Members

Status	*Muslims*		*Backward Castes*		*Scheduled Castes*	
	N	%	*N*	%	*N*	%
Emplhyed	1638	73.0	210	80.8	129	74.6
Unemployed	608	27.0	50	19.2	44	25.4
Total	2246	100.0	260	100.0	173	100.0

problem. To them, jobs in Government services and industries are signs of progress. If this is not there, their problem remains the same whatever may be numerical status in employment.

Occupations

Table 6.2 deals with the major occupations of the Backward Castes, Muslims and Scheduled Castes. Though the majority of all these groups are involved in agricultural sector, more Muslims than the Backward Castes are cultivators. But there arc more Scheduled castes than Muslims. While 28% Muslims are cultivators, Scheduled Castes account for 31% and Backward Castes for 25%. Respondents were able to offer some interesting explanation. There were more Muslims as cultivators in the past, about two decades ago, than now. Their number is on steady decline because of the Land Reforms Act, migration and partition of land, and also loss of interest in cultivation of lands for certain practical reasons. It was also narrated by some Muslims that till recently the Scheduled Castes were their tenants and labourers.

The situation is different in the case of the Scheduled Castes. They were almost agricultural labourers in the past. Ownership of land was just impossible for them because of various restrictions imposed on them. But with the change of time, particularly after independence, their conditions began to change, mostly because of the extension of protective discrimination policy in their favour. The surplus land under the Land Reforms Act is given to them. There are also some other policies of the State in their favour. The result is that the Scheduled Castes are today better placed than the Muslims.

However, compared to the Backward Castes, Muslims have generally an edge over the former as land owners inspite of the gradual decline in the number of land owners. But the Tigalas, a Backward Caste, are better farmers than the Muslims. Even with half an acre of land, the Tigalas could manage to adopt

TABLE 6.2

Distribution of the Respondents by Major Occupations

Major Occupations	*Muslims*		*Backward Castes*		*Scheduled Castes*	
	N	*%*	*N*	*%*	*N*	*%*
Cultivation	191	28.1	30	25.0	25	31.2
Agricultural Labour	161	23.7	32	26.7	30	37.5
Industry	18	2.6	18	15.0	36	37.5
Industrial labour	48	7.1	16	13.3	10	12.5
Government service	40	5.9	12	10.0	9	11.3
Business	155	22.8	10	8.3	—	—
Tailoring	55	8.1	—	—	—	—
Miscellaneous	12	1.7	2	1.7	—	—
Total	680	100.0	120	100.0	80	100.0

better agricultural practices and earn assured income. The main reason is they are hard workers unlike Muslims who are often quite lazy and indifferent.

As agricultural labourers, Muslims account for a slightly lower percentage than the Backward Castes and much lower than the Scheduled Castes. While the Muslims account for 24% as farm labourers, the Backward Castes have 27% whereas the Scheduled Castes have 37%.

To conclude, Muslims have an edge over the Backward Castes. But the Scheduled Castes are slightly better than the Muslims as cultivators. Muslims are gradually turning out to be farm labourers.

So far as industrial sector is concerned, Muslims are far below the Backward Castes and Scheduled Castes. While Muslims account for 2.6% in industries, the Backward Castes have the best position with 15% and the Scheduled Castes are better than Muslims with 7.5%. Even in industrial labour sector, Muslims are far below the Backward Castes and Scheduled Castes. While the Backward Castes and Scheduled Castes account for about 13% and 12% respectively, Muslims' share is 7%.

In Government service, the Scheduled Castes as well as the Backward Castes are much better than the Muslims. While the Muslims account for just 6%, the Scheduled Castes have 11.3% representation, followed by the Backward Castes with 10%.[1]

In business, Muslims have the best advantage with 22.8%, whereas the Backward Castes are far below with 8.3%. None of the Scheduled Caste people are involved in business. This is because of social stigma. Tailoring is the virtual monopoly of

1. These percentages do not strictly reflect the actual situation at the State level. As said earlier, only three types of Backward Castes are taken in the sample.

the Muslims. None of the Backward Castes and Scheduled Castes have entered this field.

This analysis leads to the conclusion that Scheduled Castes are much better placed than the Muslims in occupations like cultivation, industry and Government service. Excepting in the case of cultivation, Muslims are far behind the Backward Castes in other non-manual occupations. Only in business and tailoring, Muslims are better than Backward Castes as well as Scheduled Castes.

Respondents' Income

One of the major means of establishing the comparative status of Muslims is to take into account the income of both the respondents and members of the families of the groups under comparison. The comparative income of the respondents is provided in the Table 6.3.

It is seen that 61% Muslim respondents have income less than Rs. 300/- p.m. whereas 88% Backward Castes and 71% Scheduled Castes are found in this group. Further, while 19% Muslims respondents are in the mid-income range of 400—500, there are 26% Scheduled Castes and 10% Backward Castes here. It means that in this income range, Scheduled Castes are better placed than Muslims and Muslims are better than the Backward Castes.

However, Muslims account for a much better position where the income range of Rs. 500 and above is taken into consideration. There are 19% Muslims as against the negligible percentage of 2.4% Backward Castes and 2.6% Scheduled Castes. None of the Scheduled Castes have an income of Rs. 600/- and above, whereas 14% Muslims and just 1.6 Backward Castes are in this group.

The net position is that Muslims are better placed than either Backward Castes and Scheduled Castes so far income is

TABLE 6.3

Distribution of Respondents by Monthly Income

Income (in Rs.)	*Muslims*		*Backward Caste*		*Scheduled Castes*	
	N	%	*N*	%	*N*	%
Upto 100	55	7.6	15	12.5	5	6.2
100—200	165	22.9	40	33.3	20	25.0
200—300	224	31.0	50	41.8	32	40.0
300—400	70	9.7	10	8.3	18	22.5
400—500	70	9.7	2	1.7	3	3.7
500—600	33	4.7	1	0.8	2	2.6
600—700	22	3.0	1	0.8	—	—
700—800	35	4.8	1	0.8	—	—
800+	48	6.6	—	—	—	—
Total	722	100.0	120	100.0	80	100.0

concerned. What perhaps would be more interesting is to examine why Muslims remain more backward than either the Backward Castes or Scheduled Castes in general.

Monthly Family Income

There is a general feeling that income is not a problem among the Muslims. There are other factors which keep them backward. Are the Muslims better than either the Backward Castes or Scheduled Castes ? Table 6.4 provides some clue to this question.

It is seen that a vast majority of the Muslims as well as the other social groups under examination have income below Rs. 300/- per moth. In the case of Muslims, 68% do not have income exceeding Rs. 300/- Among the Backward Castes, it is 81% in this income range group. About 85% Scheduled Castes are found in this range. It means that in the lower income group, Muslims are better than the Scheduled Castes. They are also slightly better than the Backward Castes.

However, the situation changes in the middle income range between Rs. 300/- and Rs. 500/-. While Muslims are slightly better than the Scheduled Castes with 15% as against 13% among the Scheduled Castes, Backward Castes are better than the Muslims with 17%.

But in higher income group range of 500 and above, Muslims are far better than either the Backward Castes or Scheduled Castes. While 17% Muslims are found in this range, Backward Castes account for 2% and the Scheduled Castes for about 1%.

It is thus evident that the family income position of the Muslims in general is much better than the Backward Castes as well as the Scheduled Castes. This confirms the general feeling.

Land Holdings

The quantity and quality of land holdings among the three groups are indicated in table 6.5. All these three groups have

TABLE 6.4

Monthly Income of the Family

Income (in Rs.)	*Muslims*		*Backward Castes*		*Scheduled Castes*	
	N	%	*N*	%	*N*	%
Upto 100	225	13.6	50	19.2	40	23.1
100—200	521	31.4	100	38.5	60	34.7
200—300	374	22.6	60	23.1	48	27.7
300—400	154	9.3	30	11.5	20	11.7
400—500	100	6.0	15	5.8	3	1.7
500—600	55	3.3	5	1.9	2	1.1
600—700	32	1.9	—	—	—	—
700—800	61	3.7	—	—	—	—
800+	136	8.2	—	—	—	—
Total	1658	100.0	260	100.0	173	100.0

Note : 20 additional respondents included here, though not included tn the Table on occupations.

TABLE 6.5

Types and Acreage of Land Holdings

Quantity (acres)	Muslims					
	Dry land		Wet land		Garden land	
	N	%	N	%	N	%
1	2	3	4	5	6	7
Upto 1	70	33.3	20	51.3	5	83.3
1.0—2.5	80	38.1	10	25.6	—	—
2.5—5.0	40	19.1	6	15.4	—	—
5.0—10.0	15	7.1	3	7.7	1	16.7
10.0—20.0	5	2.4	—	—	—	—
Total	210	100.0	39	100.0	6	100.0

Backward Castes						Scheduled Castes					
Dry land		*Wet land*		*Garden land*		*Dry land*		*Wet land*		*Garden land*	
N	*%*	*N*	*%*	*N*	*%*	*N*	*%*	*N*	*%*	*N*	*%*
8	9	10	11	12	13	14	15	16	17	18	19
18	45.0	10	5.5	3	60.0	14	56.0	5	62.5	—	—
10	25.0	5	27.9	2	40.0	8	32.0	3	37.5	—	—
7	17.5	2	11.1	—	—	3	12.0	—	—	—	—
5	12.5	1	5.5	—	—	—	—	—	—	—	—
—	—	—	—	—	—	—	—	—	—	—	—
40	100.0	18	100.0	5	100.0	25	100.0	8	100.0	—	—

lot of similarities. A little less than one-third of Muslims, one-third of the Backward Castes and a little more than one-third of the Scheduled Castes do have dry lands. Among them, the majority are marginal farmers having dry lands not exceeding 2.5 acres. Muslims are slightly fewer than the Scheduled Castes and almost on par with the Backward Castes.

Muslims, Backward Castes and Scheduled Castes do have some amount of wet lands. But the number of such persons is extremely negligible. Further, a vast majority of these groups owning wet lands have less than one acre, thereby constituting marginal farmers. Only 6 Muslims and 5 Backward Castes have garden lands and the majority do not have such lands exceeding one acre. However, Muslims are better than the Scheduled Castes so far as the garden lands are concerned because none of the Scheduled Castes have garden lands.

It is further observed that Muslims are slightly better than the Backward Castes and much better than the Scheduled Castes so far as those who have lands in the range of 2.5 acres and above are concerned.

The entire land holding situation as analysed above places Muslims above the Backward castes and Scheduled castes. Very interesting field information was available while trying to know ihe background for this. Muslims did have plenty of land in the past, before independence, particularly in the Hyderabad-Karnataka regions. They were mostly absentee landlords. They had engaged tenants. Their accountants and clerks were Muslims, but the tenants were Hindus.

The situation began to change to the disadvvantage of the Muslims when the Land Reforms Act was introduced in Karnataka. Muslims landlords lost their lands as they were not personally cultivating the lands. On the other hand, the Scheduled Castes in particular were the beneficiaries. Under the same Act, surplus lands have to be given to the Scheduled

Castes. Thus the Scheduled Castes began to get more and more lands. While the Scheduled Castes could get some definite advantage both as tenants and landless farm labourers, Muslims lost virtually a major portion of land.

Five Year Plans

Five Year Plans have been in operation for the last four decades. Rural people are expected to take advantage of the inputs therein. But it all depends upon the awareness among the people. This comparative situation is examined with the help of data presented in table 6.6.

It is seen that even though a vast majority of the respondents of all the three groups in general are not aware of the programme under the Five Year Plans, Muslims account for a slightly higher percentage. While it is 74% among the Muslims, 69% Backward Castes and 70% Scheduled Castes are not aware of this.

Even with regard to the extent of awareness of these programmes, it is seen that Muslims are mostly far behind the other groups. While only 5% Muslims are fully aware, Backward Castes and Scheduled Castes account for 8% and 7% respectively. Similarly, while 7% Muslims are mostly aware, 10% Backward Castes and Scheduled Castes are in this category. Among those who are partly aware of the programmes, Muslims account for a slightly higher percentage when compared to the Backward Castes and Scheduled Castes.

Awareness of Economic Schemes (Animal Husbandry)

Awareness of schemes for animal husbandry among the three different groups is examined with reference to the data presented in table 6.7.

Dairy scheme is known to less number of Backward Castes and Scheduled Castes than Muslims. While 32% Backward

TABLE 6.6

Awareness of Programmes under Five Year Plans

Awareness	*Muslims*		*Backward Castes*		*Scheduled Castes*	
	N	%	*N*	%	*N*	%
1	2	3	4	5	6	7
Fully aware	36	4.9	10	8.3	6	7.5
Mostly aware	48	6.6	12	10.0	8	10.0
Partly aware	107	14.9	15	12.5	10	12.5
Not at all aware	531	73.6	83	69.2	56	70.0
Total	722	100.0	120	100.0	80	100.0

TABLE 6.7

Awareness of Economic Schemes (Animal Husbandary)

Schemes	*Muslims (N=722)*			
	Aware		*Not aware*	
	N	%	*N*	%
1	2	3	4	5
Dairy farming	610	84.5	112	15.5
Poultry farming	314	43.5	408	56.5
Sheep rearing	284	39.3	438	60.7
Bee keeping	128	17.7	594	82.3
Subsidy	379	52.5	343	47.5
B nk loans	560	77.6	162	22.4

Backward Castes (N=120)				*Scheduled Castes (N=80)*			
Aware		*Not aware*		*Aware*		*Not aware*	
N	%	*N*	%	*N*	%	*N*	%
6	7	8	9	10	11	12	13
39	32.5	81	67.5	40	50.0	40	50.0
50	41.7	70	58.3	30	37.5	50	62.5
70	58.3	50	41.7	30	37.5	50	62.5
10	8.3	110	91.7	8	10.0	72	90.0
50	41.7	70	58.3	50	62.5	30	37.5
70	58.3	50	41.7	50	62.5	30	37.5

Castes and 50% Scheduled Castes are aware of this scheme, 84% Muslims know. Poultry farming scheme is known to 4 % Muslims as against 42% Backward Caste and 37% Scheduled Castes. It means, Muslims have an edge over the Scheduled Castes. So far as sheep-rearing is concerned, Backward Castes have a much larger number with 58% awareness as against 39% among the Muslims. However, Muslims are slightly better than Scheduled Castes.

Bee keeping is not known to a vast majority of Muslims, Backward Castes and Scheduled Castes, the percentages being 82, 92 and 90 respectively. While the majority of the Scheduled Castes (62%) and also the majority of Muslims (52%) are aware of subsidy scheme, the majority of Backward Castes (58%) are not aware.

Bank loan scheme is known to the majority of the Muslims (78%), Backward castes (58%) and Scheduled Castes (62%). However, what is significant here is that the Muslims have the largest number of people aware of this scheme.

Economic Schemes (Agriculture)

In the context of rural development a number of economic schemes for development of agriculture have been introduced by the State. These schemes are meant for all sectors of the rural society in general and poorer sectors in particular. To what extent the rural people are aware of these schemes is presented in Table 6.8.

There is not much of difference among the Muslims, Backward Castes and Scheduled Castes so far as awareness of a number of economic schemes are concerned. While 38% Muslims are aware of land improvement schemes, the position is more or less similar among the Backward Castes and Scheduled Castes. Muslims account for just 20% in the case of minor irrigation, while the other groups are much better with

TABLE 6.8

Awareness of Economics Schemes (Agriculture)

	Muslims			
	Aware		*Not aware*	
	N	%	*N*	%
1	2	3	4	5
Land improvement	275	38.1	447	61.9
Minor irrigation	219	30.3	503	69.7
Crop Insurance	145	20.0	577	80.0
Hybrid varieties	428	59.3	294	40.7
Subsidy	439	60.8	283	39.2
Sericulture	266	36.8	456	63.2
Social Forestry	118	16.3	604	83.7
Bank loan	600	83.1	122	16.9

Backward Castes				Scheduled Castes			
Aware		*Not aware*		*Aware*		*Not aware*	
N	%	*N*	%	*N*	%	*N*	%
6	7	8	9	10	11	12	13
40	33.3	80	66.7	28	35.0	52	65.0
40	33.3	80	66.7	28	35.0	52	65.0
30	25.0	90	75.0	21	26.2	59	73.8
61	50.8	59	49.2	42	52.5	38	47.5
80	66.7	40	33.3	48	60.0	32	40.0
40	33.3	80	66.7	20	25.0	60	75.0
26	21.7	94	78.3	15	18.7	65	81.3
95	79.2	25	20.8	65	81.2	15	18.8

33% and 35% respectively. Crop Insurance scheme is known to 20% Muslims, 25% Backward Castes and 26% Scheduled Castes. The difference here is not at all significant.

Hybrid variety of crops is known to a majority of all the groups with Muslims having a slight edge over the other two groups. While Muslims account for 59%, in the case of others, awareness is to the extent of around 50%. Similarly, subsidy scheme is known to the majority of the three groups. But while Muslims and Scheduled Castes account for around 60%, there is awareness to the extent of 67% among the Backward Castes.

Muslims are much better than the Scheduled Castes so far as Sericulture scheme is concerned. While Muslims account for 37%, scheduled Castes have only 25% awareness. But Muslims and Backward Castes are almost on par, with the Backward Castes accounting for 33%.

Social forestry scheme is known to just 16% Muslims and 19% Scheduled Castes. The difference is just marginal. However, Backward Castes are slightly better than Muslims with 22% awareness. So far as Bank loan scheme is concerned, a vast majority of all the groups are aware of it. While Muslims are almost on par with the Scheduled Castes, Backward Castes are slightly behind the Muslims.

Employment and Wage Schemes

Some other important economic schemes of the Government are improved wages, minimum wages, equal wages for equal work and rural employment. Though these schemes are in existence for quite sometime, its awareness poses questions of doubt. Hence, the issue was brought to the notice of the respondents of various groups. The position is presented in table 6.9.

Awareness of improved wages scheme is more among Muslims (36%) than the Backward Castes (25%), but the Scheduled

TABLE 6.9

Awareness of Economic Schemes (Employment and Wages)

Schemes	*Muslims*			
	Aware		*Not aware*	
	N	%	*N*	%
1	2	3	4	5
Improved wages	262	36.3	460	63.7
Minimum wages	140	19.4	622	80.6
Equal wages for equal work	35	4.9	687	95.1
Rural employment	264	36.6	462	60.4

Backward Castes				Scheduled Castes			
Aware		*Not aware*		*Aware*		*Not aware*	
N	%	*N*	%	*N*	%	*N*	%
6	7	8	9	10	11	12	13
30	25.0	90	75.0	32	40.0	48	60.0
60	50.0	60	50.0	65	81.2	15	18.8
7	5.8	113	94.2	3	3.7	77	96.3
42	35.0	78	65.0	36	45.0	44	55.0

Castes account for a better position than Muslims with 40%. The minimum wages scheme is not known to vast majority of the Muslims (81%). Backward Castes are better with 50% awareness. Scheduled Castes are far better than Muslims.

So far as the scheme of equal wages for equal work is concerned. Muslims are in no way different from the Backward Castes and Scheduled Castes. Around 95% respondents of all the groups are unaware of this scheme. Rural employment scheme is known to more Scheduled Castes (45%) than Muslims (37%). Muslims are almost on par with the Backward Castes (35%). The net position is that by and large Scheduled Castes are much better than the Muslims, while the Backward Castes are almost on par with the Muslims.

Educational Status

The literacy status of the three groups under comparison is presented in table 6.10. It is seen that a vast majority of all the groups are illiterates. While Muslims account for 52% illiteracy, the position is slightly worse in the case of the Backward Castes (58%) and worst among the Scheduled Castes, both accounting for 72%. It means Muslims are far better than the Scheduled Castes.

Further break up of the literates into the various standards reveals that among all these groups, the majority are those who have studied upto lower primary standard only. Muslims account for 45%, Backward Castes 50% and Scheduled Castes 45%, At upper primary level, Scheduled Castes are equal to Muslims, the percentage being around 41. However, Backward Castes have a lower percentage of 30.

But at the high school level, Backward Castes are better than Muslims, percentages being 20 and 8. Scheduled Castes are slightly better than Muslims (14%).

Beyond high school, it is seen that while none of the Backward Castes and Scheduled Castes have any-one, Muslims have

TABLE 6.10

Educational Status of Respondents

Educational Status	*Muslims* N	*Muslims* %	*Backwara castes* N	*Backwara castes* %	*Scheduled castes* N	*Scheduled castes* %
A. Literary Status						
Illiterate	374	51.8	70	58.3	58	72.8
Literate	348	48.2	50	41.7	22	27.5
Total	722	100.0	120	100.0	80	100.0
B. Break up of literates						
Lower Primary	158	45.4	25	50.0	10	45.4
Upper Primary	144	41.4	15	30.0	9	40.9
High School	28	8.1	10	20.0	3	13.7
Diploma in Tech. Education	4	1.1	—	—	—	—
College	14	4.0	—	—	—	—
Total	348	100.0	50	100.0	22	100.0

had atleast 4 persons in Diploma course and 14 persons in college.

Social Legislations

Awareness of some of the important legislations is presented in table 6.11. Though a vast majority of the respondents of all the three groups are not aware of the Minimum Wages Act, Muslims account for the higher percentage with 91% as against 77% among the Backward Castes and 75% among the Scheduled Castes.

So far as awareness of Land Reforms Act is concerned, it is seen that Muslims are better placed with 39% as against the Backward Castes with 25%. But more Scheduled Castes are aware than the Muslims with 62%. This is possible because of the fact that the Scheduled Castes are the direct beneficiaries from the Land Reforms Act both as ex-tenants and farm labourers.

Bonded Labour (Abolition) Act is known to a vast majority of the Scheduled Castes with 75%. But Muslims are far behind. Only 12% Muslims are aware of this law. Even the Backward Castes are much better with 25%. The higher percentage is again due to the fact that a vast majority of the bonded labourers are Scheduled Castes.

The State has been trying to create more awareness of the importance of and procedure for registering births and deaths. But the results obtained in the study indicate Muslims as well as the Backward Castes and Scheduled Castes are mostly ignorant. Of course, Muslims account a slightly larger share of ignorance with 97% than either the Backward Castes or Scheduled Castes accounting for 90%.

A vast majority of Muslims as well as the two other groups are ignorant of the Agricultural Income Tax Act, the percentage being 90% and around. Compulsory Education Act is not

TABLE 6.11

Awareness of Social Legislations

Legislations	Muslims (N=722)			
	Aware		*Not aware*	
	N	%	*N*	%
1	2	3	4	5
Minimum Wages Act	65	9.0	657	91.0
Land Reforms Act	285	39.4	437	60.6
Bonded Labour (Abolition) Act	90	12.5	632	87.5
Registration of Births and deaths Act	25	3.4	697	96.6
Agricultural Income Tax Act	75	10.4	647	89.6
Compulsory Education Act	23	3.2	699	96.8
Special Marriage Act	16	2.2	706	97.8

Backward Castes (N=120)				Scheduled Castes (N=80)			
Aware		Not Aware		Aware		Not aware	
N	%	N	%	N	%	N	%
6	7	8	9	10	11	12	13
28	23.3	92	76.7	20	25.0	60	75.0
30	25.0	90	75.0	50	62.5	30	37.5
30	25.0	90	75.0	60	75.0	20	25.0
12	10.0	108	90.0	8	10.0	72	90.0
10	8.3	110	91.7	8	10.0	72	90.0
10	8.3	110	91.7	—	—	80	100.0
—	—	120	100.0	—	—	80	100.0

known to 97% Muslims, 92% Backward Castes and 100% Scheduled Castes. Special Marriage Act is not known to 98% Muslims and 100% Backward Castes and Scheduled Castes.

In general, it can be said that Muslims are worse than the Backward Castes and Scheduled Castes so far as awareness of social legislations is concerned.

Awareness of Health Programmes

Table 6.12 provides data on the awareness of the various health programmes. It is seen that there is a lot of agreement among all the groups. Excepting family planning where the vast majority of all the groups are aware, all the remaining programmes are not known to a vast majority.

Child care is known to only 19% Muslims, whereas Backward Castes and Scheduled Castes have better awareness with 33% and 26%. Immunization programme is also known to only 17% Muslims, while the percentage of awareness is almost double among the Backward Castes and Scheduled Castes Even with regard to dental health programme, Muslims are slightly behind the Backward Castes and almost on par with the Scheduled Castes.

Programmes to combat tuberculosis are also not known to a vast majority of the respondents. But Muslims account for a higher percentage of awareness compared to the Backward Castes and Scheduled Castes. Though only 17% Muslims are aware of this, Backward castes and Scheduled Castes account for a much lower percentage. Awareness of Cancer is only to the extent of 5% among Muslims and Scheduled Castes, while 8% of Backward Castes are aware of this.

None of the respondents know anything about the most dreaded disease, AIDS. Programmes for rehabilitation of the physically and mentally handicapped children are known to a small percentage of Muslims. However, Muslims appear to be

TABLE 6.12

Awareness of Health Programmes

Programmes	*Muslims*			
	Aware		*Not Aware*	
	N	%	*N*	%
Child Health	140	19.3	582	80.3
Immunization	120	16.6	602	83.4
Family Planning	620	85.9	102	14.1
Dental health	80	11.0	682	89.0
Tuberculosis	120	16.6	602	83.4
Cancer	40	5.5	682	94.5
AIDS	—	—	722	100.0
Physically handicapped Children	90	12.5	632	87.5
Mentally handicapped children	61	8.4	661	91.5

Backward Castes				*Scheduled Castes*			
Aware		*Not aware*		*Aware*		*Not aware*	
N	%	N	%	N	%	N	%
6	7	8	9	10	11	12	13
40	33.3	80	66.7	21	26.2	59	73.8
36	30.0	84	70.0	26	32.5	54	67.5
98	81.7	22	18.3	70	87.5	10	12.5
20	16.7	100	83.3	10	12.5	70	87.5
12	10.0	108	90.0	10	12.5	70	87.5
10	8.3	110	91.7	4	5.0	76	95.0
—	—	120	100.0	—	—	80	100.0
10	8.3	110	91.7	10	12.5	70	87.5
5	4.2	115	95.8	6	7.5	74	92.5

slightly better than the Backward Castes and almost equal to Scheduled Castes.

Social Security Measures

Awareness of Social security measures among the three groups is presented in table 6.13. Life insurance measure is not known to about three-fourth of Muslims as well as the Backward and Scheduled groups. Health Insurance scheme is not known to 90% of these groups. Muslims are on par with the Backward Castes and Scheduled castes.

Crop insurance is not known to 90% Muslims, whereas the position is slightly better among the Backward Castes and much better among the Scheduled Castes, where the percentages of not being aware are 86.7 and 62.5 respectively. It means that more Scheduled Castes are aware of crop insurance schemes than the Muslims.

But so far as animal insurance scheme is concerned, Muslims are better placed than both the Backward Castes and Scheduled Castes, While 40% Muslims are aware, it is only 25% among the Backward castes and 31% among the Scheduled Castes.

Old age pension is known to more Muslims than the Scheduled Castes and slightly less compaied to Backward Castes. Awareness is to the extent of 51% among the Muslims and 60% among the Backward Castes, while it is to the extent of 52% among the Scheduled Castes. Widow pension is known to 38% Muslims, whereas it is to the extent of 51% among the Backward Castes and 52% among the Scheduled Castes. A vast majority of all the groups are not aware of Indira Vikas Patrika. But Muslims are slightly better than Scheduled Castes, the percentage of awareness being 12 and 10 respectively However, Backward Castes are much better than Muslims with 25%. The position is similar in relation to the National Savings Certificates.

TABLE 6.13

Awareness of Social Security Measures

Measures	*Muslims*			
	Aware		*Not Aware*	
	N	%	*N*	%
1	2	3	4	5
Life Insurance	192	26.6	530	73.4
Health Insurance	60	8.3	662	91.7
Crop Insurance	70	9.7	652	90.3
Animal Insurance	289	40.0	433	60.0
Old age pension	370	51.2	352	48.8
Widow pension	275	38.1	447	61.9
Indira Vikas Patrika	90	12.5	632	87.5
National Saving Certificate	110	15.2	612	84.8

	Backward Castes				Scheduled Castes			
	Aware		Not Aware		Aware		Not Aware	
	N	%	N	%	N	%	N	%
	6	7	8	9	10	11	12	13
	28	23.3	62	76.7	18	22.5	62	77.5
	12	10.0	108	90.0	8	10.0	72	90.0
	16	13.3	104	86.7	30	37.5	50	62.5
	30	25.0	90	75.0	25	31.2	55	68.8
	72	60.0	48	40.0	42	52.5	38	47.5
	61	50.8	59	49.2	42	52.5	38	47.5
	30	25.0	90	75.0	8	10.0	72	90.0
	30	25.0	90	75.0	8	10.0	72	90 0

What emerges from the above analysis is that Muslims are generally more backward than either the castes Backward Castes or Scheduled Castes so far as the question of awareness of social Security measares are concerned. The Scheduled Castes who were virtually nothing a couple of decades ago seem to have an edge over Muslims. Even the traditional Backwards are better than Muslims.

A further probe reveals that one of the major factors responsible for this is the active role played by the voluntary organizations among the Backward Castes and Scheduled Castes. Even the officials have helped them a lot in creating better awareness, at least when compared to the Muslims.

Role of Religious Leaders

It is generally accepted that the religious leaders of Christians are involved in socio-economic development, besides religious functions. Do the religious leaders of the Muslims and Hindus also do this service? Views of the respondents are presented in table 6.14.

Only about 5% Muslims respondents say that religious leaders play a role in socio-economic development. Even then, it is only moderately useful. As high as 95% Muslims say that they do not have a role to play. Muslim repondents do not hesitate to find fault with the religions leaders who are confined to sermons within the four walls of the mosque.

The situation is slightly different in the case of the Scheduled Castes and marginally different in the case of the Backward Castes. While 100% Scheduled Castes say that the religious leaders do not play any role at all in their development, only 8.3% Backward Castes are of the opinion that the leaders play a moderate role.

A further analysis with the help of data obtained in group discussion reveals that while the Scheduled Castes hold the

TABLE 6.14

Role of Religious Leaders in Socio-Economic Development

Opinion	*Muslims*		*Backward Castes*		*Scheduled Castes*	
	N	%	*N*	%	*N*	%
Extremely useful	—	—	—	—	—	—
Moderately useful	33	4.6	10	8.3	—	—
Not at all useful	689	95.4	110	91.7	80	100.0
Total	722	100.0	120	100.0	80	100.0

Hindu religious leaders responsible for their harmful role, Muslims just say "that it is unfortunate that our religious leaders remain mum on development issues". The general opinion is more or less common to the Muslims and Scheduled Castes and even to the Backward castes, though the opinion is slightly different.

Opinion about Comparative Backwardness

The above said analysis indicates the relative status of Muslims when compared to the Backward Castes and Scheduled Castes. But the question is, are the Muslims aware of their status in comparison with the Backward Castes and Scheduled Castes in particular and all the caste groups in general? If so, what is their opinion in matters relating to educational and economic conditions? This is examined with reference to the data presented in table 6.15.

The groups compared are : Hindus in general, Brahmins, Lingayats, Vokkaligas, Backward Castes and Scheduled castes in particular. Eighty three percent respondent feel that they are worse than the Hindus in general in education. While 16.9% say that they are not able to assess the situation, there is none who would say that the Muslims are better than or equal to the Hindus.

Caste reference makes the position still clearer. None of the respondents feel that they are better than or equal to the Brahmins, Lingayats and Vokkaligas. A vast majority of them exceeding 80% are of the opinion that they are worse than all these caste groups. A small percentage remains neutral.

But the opinion of respondents is slightly different when they compare themselves with Backward Castes and Scheduled Castes in matters relating to education. Twenty six percent respondents' opinion is that they are better than Backward castes, whereas 22% feel they are equal. Those who feel they are worse account for 35% and the rest remain neutral. But

TABLE 6.15

Opinion of Respondents on Comparative Backwardness

Groups compared	Education (N=722)							
	Better		Equal		Worse		Do not know	
	N	%	N	%	N	%	N	%
1	2	3	4	5	6	7	8	9
Hindus in General	—	—	—	—	600	83 1	122	16.9
Brahmins	—	—	—	—	700	97.0	22	3.0
Lingayats	—	—	—	—	611	84.6	111	15.4
Vokkaligas	—	—	—	—	621	86.0	101	14.0
Backward Castes	186	25.8	160	22.2	256	35.4	120	16.6
Scheduled Castes	196	27.1	104	14.4	321	44.5	101	14.0

Economic (N=722)							
Better		*Equal*		*Worse*		*Donot know*	
N	%	*N*	%	*N*	%	*N*	%
10	11	12	13	14	15	16	17
—	—	—	—	582	80.6	140	19.4
—	—	—	—	650	90.0	72	10.0
—	—	11	1.5	601	83.2	110	15.3
—	—	60	8.3	600	83.1	62	8.6
156	21.6	135	18.7	349	48.3	82	11.4
200	27.7	190	26.4	310	42.9	22	3.0

more Muslims feel that they are worse than Scheduled Castes. While 35% feel they are worse than Backward castes, a slightly higher percentage with 44% feel that they are worse than Scheduled Castes. While 27% feel that they are better than Scheduled Castes, 14% say that they are equal.

A little more than 80% respondents say that they are worse than the higher caste Hindus in economic status. While 48% say that they are worse than the Backward castes, 43% say so when compared to the Scheduled castes. Nearly 28% feel that they are better than Scheduled Castes and 26% feel they are equal. One important point here is that while 11% respondents remain neutral so far as the Backward castes are concerned, only 3% remain neutral when asked to comment on the Scheduled Castes. This reduced number of the respondents who remain neutral so far as the Scheduled Castes are concerned, makes a lot of difference in the opinion of the respondents whether they are better or worse than the Backward castes or Scheduled castes.

This analysis makes it clear that the Muslims feel in general that even the Backward Castes and Scheduled Castes are better than them in educational as well as economic status. In group discussion, the reasons which made them say so were assessed and are presented here.

Housing Schemes

Muslims say that the housing schemes of the Government have not provided them any advantage. Most of them are living in old houses, often built by their fathers and grandfathers. Conditions of the houses have deteriorated. Only a handful of them have either built new houses or renovated. The rest suffer from many handicaps. The large size family poses a big problem. Houses do not have basic facilities. The houses of Muslims are segregated as is true with Hindu social groups. Muslims feel that the Government is encouraging the Scheduled Castes with Janata housing schemes, whereas Muslims are totally neglected.

Another interesting point that emerged is the feeling that the houses of the Muslims are worsening, while the houses of the Scheduled Castes in particular are improving during the last two decades.

Water

Water is required both for drinking and irrigation purposes. The recent attempts of the State to provide bore wells to the rural people have not generally helped the Muslims. Borewells are drilled mostly in Scheduled Castes areas or nearer to their area which would not help Muslims in particular to fetch water. Irrigation facilities too have not reached Muslim farmers. The existing wells need to be deepened, but the State policy does very little service according to them.

Bank Loans

Muslims feel that generally it would be too difficult to obtain loans from the banks. The rigid conditions and indifference towards the minorities have disillusioned the Muslims. Knowledgeable Muslims do feel that whatever special treatment the Bank managements have adopted for the Scheduled Castes be extended to the Muslims too. They say that the Backward Castes people have better access to the banks than the Muslims.

Bureaucracy

Muslims feel that while the Muslim officers are not helpful to their development, the non-Muslims officers in general have no special interest in Muslim development. Many officers take special interest in the development of Scheduled castes in particular. Even the Backward caste people are better attended to than the Muslims. This indifference of bureaucratic role is both in regard to officers and village level functionaries.

Leadership

The respondents feel disappointed with Muslim leadership. They express their appreciation of the role of the Hindu leadership to tackle the socio-economic problems. The Scheduled caste leadership as well as Backward caste leadership is at least relatively beneficial for these groups when compared to Muslim leadership.

Women's Status

While in general Muslim masses are not clear about the comparative status of Muslim women, knowledgeable Muslims could give their opinion. They feel that the social status of Muslim women is definitely better than that of the Scheduled Caste women. Though conscious of the fact that Muslim society does not generally encourage social mobility among Muslim women, they do feel that their women do not suffer from social taboos. Educationally also Muslim women are better than Scheduled Caste as well as Backward Caste women. However, Muslims feel that Muslim women are neglected by both Muslim leaders as well as the State. If facilities extended to the Scheduled Caste women are also given to Muslim women, there could be some progress, according to Muslim leaders.

Employment

Muslims feel that they are hard hit in employment matters. Self-employment suffers for want of necessary facilities. Government service as well as service in public undertakings are not helpful to the Muslims. On the other hand, Scheduled Castes who were once the worst sufferers are now coming up. They are far better than the Muslims. Even the Backward Castes have an edge over the Muslims, according to Muslim leaders.

Land Holdings

Muslims had plenty of lands in the past. Today they are

losing their lands. They say that the Scheduled Castes have better access to the land grant policies of the State. Even Backward castes are better than the Muslims. What Muslims say is that there is downward mobility among Muslims as against upward mobility among the Scheduled Castes and Backward castes.

Development Corporations

Both Muslims and Scheduled Castes have Development Corporations. Muslim leaders say that while the SC/ST Development Corporation has a permanent and durable status, besides adequate funds, power, role and attention of the State, Minority Development Corporation suffers for want of all this. There is definite progress made by SC/ST Development Corporation, while very little has been done by the Minority Development Corporation.

Response to Development

Muslims are lazy and indifferent to development. Scheduled Castes and Backward castes are far better, atleast relatively. There is no imagination or desire to get more and more involved in development processes. Muslim leaders say that Scheduled Castes and Backward castes are definitely better. They feel that at this rate, Muslims will be the worst sufferers in course of time.

Child Development

There are many programmes for child development such as pre-primary education, Integrated Child Development Schemes, immunization, nutritious food, general health care, etc. Muslims feel that the Scheduled Castes are better placed in all these areas of developmental activities. Government has special programmes for these people. There are agencies to monitor and evaluate the implementation of these schemes. Even the position of the Backward castes is slightly better.

The status of Muslim children is going down, while that of the Scheduled Castes and Backward Castes is moving up.

Factionalism

Another area of comparison is the solidarity issue. Muslims feel that they are disunited and suffer from factionalism. Development suffers from this. They do not have organizations to create awareness and promote development, whereas the Scheduled Castes and Backward Castes are relatively better placed. The Scheduled Castes in particular, have the charisma of Baba Saheb Ambedkar and they are getting united and reinforced, whereas the Muslim masses have no such charismatic leaders to unite them and encourage development.

The infighting among Muslims is presented through a few case studies.

Demand for Rights

Muslim development suffers partly because either the demands of Muslims are not relevant or because there is the organized effort to stall their development. The general demands of the Muslims centre round mosque, burial ground and language. Muslim leadership is generally confined to these areas which have nothing to do with development. Rural masses are more bothered about inputs for development. But no one cares for the rightful demands.

In contrast, according to Muslim knowledgeable persons, Scheduled castes in particular are better placed. They claim facilities and privileges as a matter of right. Government comes under attack and yields to them. Even Backward castes have an edge over the Muslims. They receive better attention, though not as much as the Scheduled Castes receive.

Case-studies Relating to Factionalism

One of the major reasons for Muslim backwardness is factionalism. Infighting over trivial issues came to surface in many villages. These issues were still burning in some areas. A few such instances are illustrated here to prove the point that Muslims generally are not development oriented but often are dispute oriented.

(1) *Case Study of Mosque Committees*

In a village of Arasikere taluk, Muslims constitute a minority group. About one-fourth of the population belongs to Muslims and the rest are Hindus. There are 60 Muslim families. They are backward. Most of them are manual labourers and a few marginal farmers. The majority of them are illiterates. Their participation in development processes is negligible.

Even in such distressing conditions, there are two groups, vertically divided with hostile attitudes. One group has 20 families and the other group has 40 families. The majority group attempts to exercise its hold over the minority group whenever and wherever possible. The dispute originated due to the constitution of the mosque committee some years ago. There is neither co-operation nor coordination between the two groups.

One day an old man died. He was of the minority group. His relatives wanted the coffin (Janaza) to take the body from the house to the graveyard. They also needed the services of the priest. Since the mosque committee was dominated by the majority group, the committee decided neither to give the coffin nor send the priest. The minority group was not bothered about the priest since they could get one from the neighbouring village. But they needed the coffin. This plea did not materialise. The minority group sought the intervention of the local Hindu leaders, particularly the Mandal Panchayat Chief.

The majority group did not cherish the intervention of the non-Muslims in their religious affairs. But they did not have courage to oppose their intervention. A compromise formula was worked out, almost a face-saving device. The majority group demanded clearance of arrears towards the mosque maintenance subscription from the family of the dead.

Every family had to pay a monthly contribution of Rs 5/- towards the mosque maintenance fund. The minority group decided not to pay since the differences between them became serious over the constitution of the mosque committee. There was none from the group of the minorities on the committee. So they decided not to pay the contribution. This was pending for some years.

When the Hindu leaders intervened and brought pressure, the majority group agreed to give the coffin but subject to the condition that the family cleared the arrears. Since time was short for burial, the minority group agreed to pay and got the coffin. But the side effect of this ugly incident was still green in the minds of the minority group. There were no symptoms of reconciliation and integration.

On the other hand, this incident further alienated the minority group which was preparing to boycott the mosque and go to a neighbouring village for special prayers on Fridays.

When the research team met the two groups and tried to get detailed information, the majority group gave certain firm replies. The conversation that took place between the Director of the Research team and the local leader of Muslims is as follows :

Director : Is is true that the Coffin was not given until payment was made ?

Leader : Yes, it is true.

Director : Is it not un-Islamic ?

Leader : May be, I could not help.

Director : Was there no alternative remedy ?

Leader : No

Director : Was it not possible for you to release the Coffin first and collect the arrears later on ?

Leader : No Sir, this was the best opportunity. Otherwise, we had to wait for another death case to recover the arrears.

Director : Is payment of mosque contribution compulsory ?

Leader : Yes Sir, otherwise, how to manage the mosque

Director : What do you do if people do not give contribution ?

Leader : We will impose social boycot and refuse to give services of the mosque

Director : Is it true that the non-Muslim leaders brought pressure on you ?

Leader : Yes, but we yielded only when the minority group agreed to pay the arrears.

Director : Is it not an insult to Muslims when the non-Muslims know about the behaviour of Muslims and internal conflicts.

Leader : Yes Sir, But we are not responsible. The other group should also realise.

Director : Is it not possible to sit across the table and sort out differences ?

Leader : Perhaps, yes. But who will take the initiative ?

Director : Can we try ?

Leader : Yes Sir, you may.

Then a meeting was arranged between the two groups. The Director of the Research team took the initiative and explained to them about developmental programmes and the advantages of united efforts. There was good response. They were made to understand that internal differences and fighting would keep Muslims backward. There seemed to be some ray of hope.

(2) Mosque Committee of Ahmedpur

Mosque Committees are often full of internal factions and fighting. It is very strange that the sacredness and sanctity of the Mosque would be in danger because of selfish and greedy members of the Committees. There are generally two groups. The President of the Mosque becomes a dictator. He does not follow rules of law. Democratic approach is not known and practised even though Islam has provided the best democratic frame for self-governance. One significant instance of how the Mosque Committee affects oneness among the people is illustrated here.

In Ahmadpur village, there were two groups among the members of the Mosque Committee. This is a small village with 90% Muslim population. They are all generally related to one another. The leaders of the two factions are cousins. The main reason for dispute was about the secretaryship. Since one group had the Secretary from among its members, the other group decided to boycott the activities of the mosque. Of course, it is conceded that the Mosque Committee was not involved in any developmental activities. It could atleast provide a common forum for people to meet and exchange views.

But it was not so. The two factions would not sit together, nor would they attend any programme if the other group is present. Even when some one invites people for a social function, care was taken to see that the members of one of the two groups did not attend the functions if the other group was present.

When approached, elderly persons were sore over the new trends of exclusiveness and factions among the youths. These elderly persons pleaded their inability to patch up the differences. They said, 'These days youngsters would not care for elders. Our own sons do not respect our words. How can we intervene and bring oneness among the people. Our boys have become anti-Islamic in their social behaviour'.

Women were more disappointed. They had no enimity among themselves. Women of both the groups would mix freely. They did not approve the attitudes of the youngsters. When asked whether they could advice the youths, they said that they did their best, but miserably failed. They said that if the youths are made to know Islamic spirit of understanding and oneness, then only some changes for better could be expected. They were not happy with what was going on among the members of the mosque committee.

The construction of the mosque building had been stopped for some time because of the internal factions. Everyone admitted that it was a sin to do so. God would not spare them. This is how Muslims of a small village remained divided.

(3) *Case-study of Co-operative Society*

There were some efforts to have co-operative functioning for the benefit of realars. In one village a society called Hindustan Realers Co-operative Society was started 8 years ago. There were 120 members. It worked well for some time. Realers would take loan and deliver thread to the market. But internal factions started taking place. Money that was received was misused One group approached the Court and thus the whole movement for co-operative efforts got stalled.

People involved in dairy activities do like to have unions. But it was not possible because factions were too many. Lack of unity is a great hindrance for development. Every one, every group was critical of the other.

When Better

Respondents were asked to comment on the present social situation compared to the past. As regards youths, the elders would say that youths in the past behaved better, were more responsible and responsive. There was none trying to motivate the youths for better behaviour and participation. But today the youth power is misused and problematic. They are arrogant. They have no values and are self-centered. They rarely listen to the elders.

Case study of Rashid and Hanuma

Rashid is a youngman aged 30 years. His father, Ghulam, is a middle aged farmer with 10 acres of dryland and 4 acres of wet land. While 50% of this was inherited by Ghulan from his father, the remainning 50% was purchased by him. He had a tenant, Muniga. The relationship between the two is cordial and one of master-servant. Muniga is a Scheduled Caste.

When the Land Reforms Act was introduced. Muniga was made to file his petition before the Land Tribunal. He was reluctant in the beginning on moral grounds. But finally he filed. This had a shocking effect on Ghulam. He told Muniga that he did a wrong. Munigı felt bad and gave excuses. Finally, the position that emerged was that Ghulam got two acres of dryland and one acre of wet land and the rest went in favour of Muniga. Ghulam would have lost even this much. The Scheduled Caste people in the village managed to persuade Muniga not to claim this much of land so that his master could retain it. Muniga yielded gracefully.

The economic conditions of Ghulam started deteriorating as his big family could not be maintained now. His son Rashid did not receive education beyond upper primary. He could not get much from the land because he had to share with his brothers. He became a pseudo tenant of a dominant caste-Hindu.

Muniga's economic status began to improve in due course. He got loan from the bank. He received inputs regularly for agricultural development. His son Hanuma who was later on called Hanumanthappa had received education only upto primary IV standard. But he became a progressive farmer. His economic status began to improve very much. He was far superior to Rashid. Once Rashid wanted some money urgently to meet his father's medical bill. He did not want to go to caste Hindus. He approached Hanuma. Hanuma felt bad because he knew that Rashid was the son of his father's master a few years ago. He obliged Rashid.

Both Ghulam and Rashid felt bad because they had to approach a Scheduled Caste person for help. The father said "this is our fate. The time has changed". "Master becomes servant and servant becomes master". He also said "I am not angry with the Scheduled Castes. They have suffered enough. Let them come up. But what about us, Muslims ? Why the Government wants us to suffer ? When our land is taken away, should not the Government give atleast a job to my son ?"

Case-Study of Rahim and Satya

Rahim and Satya were classmates in primary school of a village. While Rahim's father was a shop-keeper, Satya's father was a farm labourer. Economically, Rahim was better placed. Satya suffered economically and also socially because he was a Scheduled Caste.

Rahim left the school when he was just 12 years and had completed primary IV standard. There was a communal riot in the village because of wide spread riot in the nearby town. The shop of Rahim's father was totally gutted by some Hindus. Rahim's father could not recover and therefore, he wanted his son to leave the school. Rahim was employed by a Muslim Sericulturist in the same village. He was earning around fifteen rupees a day.

Satya was not a bright student. His parents were totally illiterates. He got all facilities from the Government for his education. He was lucky. His father got two acres of land from the Government under the Land Reforms Act. A part of the surplus land was given to him. Satya's relative was a member of the Dalit Sangharsh Samiti. This relative influenced the Bank Manager for loan. With this loan, Satya's father started improving the land. In 5 years, land started yielding better income.

Satya could get better encouragement from his father. He got through his primary education in the village and then moved to the town for High School and Bangalore City for college education. He completed his B.Sc degree in Sericulture and became an extension guide. He got posted to his own taluk.

One day he arranged a meeting of farm labourers and small/marginal farmers in his village. The village Patel was the Chief Guest.

While making a list of those who attended the meeting, he stopped his childhood friend, Rahim. He felt very happy. He went to him and expressed his happiness. But Rahim was avoiding because of his shabby clothes, unshaven face and inferiority complex. Satya was neatly dressed and appeared to be more cultured. He felt sad. After the meeting, he went to the house of Rahim and met his parents. They could not recognize him first. But when the son introduced Satya to the parents, they felt glad. They did no mind Satya entering the main room which was not allowed for the Harijans. They offered him tea and praised him.

Satya told the parents that had they also allowed Rahim to study, he too would have become an official. Rahim's father nodded his head and said 'Yes, my boy. Your father was poor, but tried to educate you. See my son. His father was relatively better placed, but did not educate his son. Today, times have changed. For my mistake, my son suffers."

Comparative Position of Muslims in Different Villages

The conditions of Muslims differ from one category of village to another category of village, as observed during the field work. There are 3 categories of villages which have a bearing on Muslim development. These are :

(1) Villages with 100% Muslim population.

(2) Villages with majority Muslim population.

(3) Villages with majority Hindu population.

When the socio-economic conditions of the Muslims are compared with those of the backward castes and the Scheduled Castes in these categories of villages, significant differences are found. The degree of awareness of various programmes for development, the extent of participation in the process of development and responses to development differ sharply from one category of villages to another category of villages.

In such villages where Muslims are 100% or almost 100%, the conditions of Muslims are very bad. They are more backward than the Backward Castes as well as the Scheduled Castes. General awareness of the programme of the State is not generally found. But on the other hand, in Muslim majority villages, as well as Hindu majority villages the conditions are far better.

The main reasons are : (1) The village functionaries have better access to the Hindus than to the Muslims. Thus, when the Hindus of a village are motivated for development and schemes for development are made known to them, even the Muslims get the advantage. Secondly, in many villages the Hindu leadership is useful to Muslims. There is an effective social interaction between the Hindus and the Muslims in some areas of activities and for some reasons. These interactions have effective influence on the Muslims. This leads to some amount of participation in developmental activities, besides creation of awareness.

As discussed earlier, Muslim villages are generally known for fighting and non-cooperation among Muslims themselves. On the other hand, in the Hindu villages there is better understanding and concerted efforts for development. Thus, even the Scheduled Castes and Backward Castes are relatively better than Muslims in taking advantage of the developmental inputs under the Five Year Plans. These observations are true not only in the case of the adult males but also in the case of adult females and children.

CHAPTER VII

Summary, Conclusions and Recommendations

Objectives

The current study on "Planning Processes and Muslim Responses in Rural Karnataka" is a follow-up study made earlier in two districts of Karnataka. The main objectives of this study are :

1. To take stock of the economic and educational conditions of rural Muslims ;
2. To find out the awareness of the various development programmes under the Five Year Plans among Muslims;
3. To study the status of Muslim women ;
4. To make a comparative study of Muslims of North Karnataka and Old Mysore State, and
5. To examine the status of Muslims in comparison with the Scheduled Castes and Backward Castes.

Research Design

Unlike the pilot study on "Muslims in the Process of Rural Development", the present study is representative in character of the whole state with certain limitations. Four districts from North Karnataka and four districts from Old Mysore regions were selected based on the concentration of Muslim population. From each district two villages were selected.

The total sample included 1042 respondents of which 120 were Muslim women and 200 were Hindus. While generally heads of the families were selected on proportionate sampling basis.

Information was gathered both through primary source and secondary source. The main instrument is used are interview schedules, group discussions, and non-participant observation. The data were edited, processed and tabulated manually. Simple statistical tools like percentages were used to analyse the date quantitatively. To some extent qualitative analysis is also done. The entire data are organized and presented in seven chapters.

A. Economic Conditions

(*i*) *Employment* : The study reveals that unemployment is not a problem among the rural Muslims. A vast majority of the Muslims are involved in agriculture. Among these people involved in agriculture, a slightly higher percentage of the respondents are cultivators as against farm labourers. A vast majority of the Muslim women who are working as farm labourers are confined to family circles or known Muslims. Because of cultural barriers, they avoid working on the farm of non-Muslims. However, where poverty is acute, they have no option but to work with any individual or group and anywhere.

Though more respondents are involved in cultivation of land, the situation is slightly different in the case of family-members. There is a higher percentage of family members involved in farm labour than in actual cultivation. Further, more females than males are found working as farm labourers. The gap between the male and female farm labourers is less in North Karnataka than in old Mysore area.

The involvement of Muslims in rural industries is marginal. The situation is almost identical in both North Karnataka and Old Mysore area. However, the respondents recognize the importance of rural industries for development. Muslims are also involved in industrial labour, though not in good number. There are slightly more females than males. Further there are not only more industrial labourers but also more females in North Karnataka region. Tailoring is another important occupation of the rural Muslims. So far as business is concerned the situation is that Muslims are involved in this occupation which has been there from generation to generation. Even women are involved. Shops are generally attached to the houses and this enables women to take care of business when their men-folk are absent. In North Karnataka region, both men and women are involved in business.

Government service is generally sought for by Muslims. The percentage of Muslim respondents in Government service comes to just six. Among the family members it is nearly 8%. The gap between the number of males and females is narrow. More Muslim women are found in Government service in North Karnataka than Old Mysore area and this difference is generally due to the fact that there are more Ayas working in schools.

(ii) *Income* : The ultimate economic status of any group or individual would very much depend upon income. The condition of Muslims is very bad. A vast majority of the respondents do not have income exceeding Rs. 300 per month. There is not much difference between the Old Mysore region and North Karnataka though the situation is slightly better in the former area.

Among the members of the family also, the situation is more or less similar. About 68% of them do not have income exceeding Rs. 300/-. Fifty six per cent males and 85% females do not have income more than Rs. 300 per month. The income position of the family in not encouraging, particularly among the females. The situation is worse in North Karnataka than in Old Mysore area.

(iii) *Loans* : It is observed that Muslims generally resort to loans. There does not seem to be much hesitation in their minds. Nearly 72% of them have taken loan. Fifty per cent have taken loan not exceeding Rs. 1000/-. More Muslims of Old Mysore region than North Karnataka have taken loans.

What is more distressing is that loans are generally taken for non-constructive purposes. Taking loan *per se* need not be a sign of discouragement. But when the majority take loans for consumable purposes such as marriage and family maintenance, the situations causes alarm. Only 27% have taken loan development purposes like animal husbandry, agriculture, for etc. The extent and purpose of loans are more or less similar in both the regions.

Another important point that needs attention is the source from where loan is taken. Loans from the banks or societies do not pose danger. But loans from private parties, particularly from the money lenders would definitely result in problems. It is seen that friends and money lenders constitute the major source. Nearly 60% take loans from them. Landlords also play a notable part. Sixteen per cent respondents have taken loans from the landlords. What was very significant here is that the landlords who happen to be Hindus do not make a distinction between Hindus and Muslims while giving loans. Though atleast 11% take loans from the banks, Muslims are generally not happy with the banks. No significant differences were found between the two regions.

(iv) *Land Holdings* : Nearly 60% Muslims have lands. But they are generally of poor quality. A vast majority have dry lands. Some of them do have wet lands and garden lands. But such people are extremely limited. Further, nearly three-fourths of them are marginal farmers, not having more than 2.5 acres. There is not much difference between the two regions, though Old Mysore area is slightly better.

Land ownership pattern has undergone significant change during the last two decades, much faster during the last five years. A vast majority of the land owners have land inherited from their fathers and only 30% have purchased. Muslims feel that Government has done very little to help them get and improve lands. They also say that the Scheduled Castes are in a better position.

(v) *Child Labour* : Child labour is a significant feature of the Muslims in both the regions. There are more male child labourers in Old Mysore region, whereas more female child labourers are found in North Karnataka region. While 56% male child labourers are employed for wages, 43% female child labourers are employed for wages. Fifty four per cent childrens are below 14 years and 19% below 10 years. The position is worse in north Karnataka region. A vast majority of the child labourers are illiterates, both original and reverted, Further, nearly 78% are employed in agriculture and animal husbandry.

B. Educational Status

Among the respondents 52% are illiterates. There is sharp variation between the North Karnataka region and Old Mysore region. While 65% are illiterates in North Karnataka region, there are 42% illiterates in Old Mysore region. Among the literates as high as 87% have had only upto primary level, particularly upto lower primary. Higher education is neglected. North Karnataka is more backward than Old Mysore region.

Nearly 60% respondents are drop-outs. There are more drop-outs in Old Mysore region (70%) than in North Karnataka region (60%). But in North Karnataka region there are more drop-outs at lower levels than in Old Mysore region. Poverty is the main reason for drop-outs. Since there are no opportunities for school drop-outs, there are about 47% reverted illiterates. The position is worse in North Karnataka region.

There is a correlation between literacy and occupational pattern. Among the cultivators, there are 53% literates, while among the farm labourers 61% are illiterates. Among the industrial labourers and businessmen there are more illiterates, whereas among the respondents involved in industries and tailoring, there are more literates (67%). However, in general they have studied upto Primary standard.

Education depends upon income as revealed in the study. There are more illiterates among those who have lower income. In the middle income range group there are 68% literates. While in the mid-income range group 46% have studied upto Upper Primary in the Upper income group, the position is still better with high school education.

Literacy among Children: Fifty one per cent children are literates. Girls are slightly better with 53% than boys with 49%. The position is better in Old Mysore region. There are more illiterates in North Karnataka region both among boys and girls. While among the literates there are 55% children with lower Primary level, those who have had Upper primary level account for 34%. Among the illiterates, there are 57% original illiterates and 43% reverted illiterates. Though the position is similar among boys and girls, there is a higher percentage of reverted illiterates among the girls. There is no difference between the Old Mysore region and North Karnataka region.

There are four major reasons for the poor response among children to education. These are lack of separate schools for girls, financial problems, involvement of girls in domestic works and lack of Urdu schools. Drop-outs among children is another serious problem of education. Both boys and girls drop-out, but more boys drop-out than girls.

Parents have different opinion about the types of education. While both secular and theological education are stressed, among those who want secular education for children, 58% desire beyond Upper Primary level. To be very specific, while 34% desire High School education, 24% desire College education. Among those who desire theological education 89% desire basic education, while only 11% desire proficiency level.

Different reasons are assigned for educating children. For Primary education, jobs, security, letter writing, reading stories and religious books form the need. For High school education the needs are : jobs and acquisition of knowledge. While High school education is needed for boys to get jobs, parents desire this for girls to enable them to adjust themselves to different social situation after marriage.

The rural education suffers from many handicaps. The respondents allege a few major reasons such as irregularity among teachers. Lack of control over teachers, lack of adequate and proper buildings, collusion between Inspectors of Schools and the teachers, and lack of basic facilities.

Adult education suffers heavily in both the areas for various reasons as inconvenient timings, places, nature of contents of the course, male teachers, etc.

Though the Government is trying to educate the parents about the relevance of age of children for admission purposes, it is seen that the people are not aware of minimum age both for the purpose of voluntary and compulsory education. No documentary evidences are generally available. This is also not insisted upon generally as otherwise admission would become a problem.

C. Awareness

Awareness of the various schemes and procedures that the State has formulated for the benefit of the people if the pre-requisite for participation in developmental processes. Therefore, the question of awareness among the rural Muslims was taken up. It was found that three-fourths of them are not at all aware of the programmes. Even among those who are aware of the programmes, a vast majority have only partial knowledge. Though in general there is no difference between Old Mysore region and North Karnataka region, the former is slightly better.

Source of information even among the people with limited knowledge is also equally important. While 10% respondents say that Muslim Officers gave them the information, 11% refer to Hindu Officers. Muslims say that Hindu political leaders play a better role in educating the Muslims directly or indirectly. Similar views are expressed in regard to the role of the organizations. There is not much difference between the Old Mysore and North Karnataka region.

Muslims are highly critical of the Muslim Officers and leaders who either feel shy or remain indifferent. Hindus are much better, according to them. Wherever Hindus are dominant Muslims have had some advantage. Where Muslims are numerically dominant, their conditions are bad, mostly because of internal group conflicts and factionalism

Programme wise awareness is presented in brief. Excepting adult education, other educational programmes are not known to a vast majority of the Muslims. There is no difference between Old Mysore region and North Karnataka region. Integrated Child Development Scheme (ICDS) is virtually unknown. There is better awareness for adult education programmes, even though full awareness is not there. Vocational education is not known to 80%. Sixty three per cent are not aware of population education. Those who are aware of, have only partial awareness. A vast majority are no aware of health education. However, the position is better in Old Mysore region.

Land improvement schemes and minor irrigation schemes are not known to vast majority. Even those who are aware of have only partial knowledge. Crop insurance scheme is not known to 80%. However, Old Mysore region is better. Hybrid varieties are known to majority of the respondents. But they have mostly partial knowledge. There is no difference between Old Mysore region and North Karnataka region.

Sericulture is not known to the majority. However, Old Mysore region is much better. Dairy scheme is known to 85%. But people have mostly partial knowledge. Though there is not much difference between the two regions, Old Mysore region is slightly better. New varieties like broilers are not known to 56%. Old Mysore region is much better. Similarly sheep rearing, and bee keeping schemes are not known to majority. But Old Mysore region is better.

Subsidy scheme is known to 52%. But the majority have partial knowledge. Old Mysore region is better. Bank loan scheme is known only to 22% majority have partial knowledge. Old Mysore region is better. Three-fourths of the people are not aware of employment and wage schemes. Even among those who are aware of most of them have partial knowledge. Old Mysore region is better than North Karnataka region. A vast majority are not aware of the Min mum Wages Act. Nearly 95% are not aware of 'equal wage for equal work'.

There is no difference between the Old Mysore region and North Karnataka region.

So far as health schemes are concerned, it is seen that only 19% are aware of child health programmes. Similarly, only 17% are aware of immunization scheme. Eleven percent are aware of dental health scheme. In all these cases, Old Mysore region is better than North Karnataka region.

Family planning scheme is known to 86%. There is no difference between the two regions. Though tuberculosis, a deadly disease, has been in existence for a long time, 86% of the respondents are not aware of the schemes to prevent or cure it. Similarly, 87% do not known the various programmes for rehabilitation of the handicapped children. While 94% are not aware of cancer detection and curative schemes, none knows anything about AIDS. The social situation is similar in both the regions.

The State has created a Minority Development Corporation to enable minorities secure some financial assistance for economic development. About 80% of the Muslims are not aware of the very existence of this corporation in both the regions.

The Minority Commission is known to 44% Muslims. Its awareness is better in Old Mysore region though both the Chairman of this Commissions were from North Karnataka region. Twenty Point Economic Programme is not known to 98% Muslims. None of the Muslims are aware of the 15 Point Programmes for the development of minorities.

Wakf Development Corporation can assist the Muslims in many ways. This Corporation is widely known. About 71% Muslims are aware of this.

Knowledge about Muslim socio-religious organizations is slightly better. Muslim League is known to 41%. Old Mysore region is better than North Karnataka region. Similarly, Baitul maal is known to 46% and Old Mysore region is better. Jamaat-e-Islamic, Al-Ameen Trust and Tablique-Jammat, are known to a vast majority. Mosque committees are known to almost all respondents. More Muslims know Jamaat-e-Islami and Al-Ameen Trust in Old Mysore region than in North Karnataka region. So far as mosque committees and Tabliq-e-Jamaat are concerned, North Karnataka region is better.

Islamic principles of development are not known to 63%. Old Mysore region is better than North Karnataka region. Minimum Wages Act is not known to 91%. The much published Land Reforms Act and Bonded Labour (Abolition) Act are known to 40% and 13% respectively. Old Mysore region is better. Laws relating to Registration of Births and Deaths and Compulsory Education are not known to 97%. There is no difference between the two regions. While the Special Marriage Act is known to only 2%, Muslim Personal Law is known to 7% only. There is no difference between the two regions.

Social security measures are also generally not known to Muslims. Life Insurance is known to 27%, health insurance to 8%, Crop insurance to 10% and animal insurance to 40%. In all these cases, Old Mysore region is better than North Karnataka region.

Old-age pension is, however, known to 51%. Old Mysore region is significantly better than North Karnataka region. Similarly, widows pension is known to 62% and Old Mysore region is much better than North Karnataka region. While Indira Vikas Patrika is known to 12%, National Savings Certificate Scheme is known to 15%. In both these cases Old Mysore region is better.

The majority of the Muslims of both the regions are not aware of the various Boards and Corporations set up by the Government for development purpose. However, 66% are aware of Mandal Panchayats in both the regions.

D. Status of Women

Women can play a great role in socio economic development. But their resources are generally not identified and utilized by men. Unnecessary restrictions are placed on them. When this is the general situation, what about Muslim women ? The study reveals that Muslim women are almost neglected.

Muslim women do like to work and earn for the family. While 58% women do not want to work on the farm as labourers, 25% women do need jobs on the farm. These are the women who are put to lot of economic hardship. When they face acute poverty and helplessness they are bound to take up jobs outside even though in general such jobs are discouraged.

Cottage industries are desired by 62% women. They are quite enthusiastic. They are aware of the reasons. They say that family care and regular income are assured, besides social image. Women are prepared to take up any industry which has a market.

Women are not against taking loans. Fifty seven per cent of them say that loan is needed, but they realize that reckless loans would do great damage to family economy. Similarly, 67% women are in favour of land holdings as this would enable them to work on their own land and help the family. They also favour training for understanding and developing skills. Fifty per cent desire adult education. Training in cottage industries is desired by 62%. Similarly, 50% want training in dairy and 42% in sericulture.

Social participation of Muslim women is examined with reference to a few sociological variables. Eighty four percent women say that they are not consulted in economic matters by their men-folk. Only 17% say that they are consulted some times. In educational matters, 50% women say that are not at all consulted. Twentyone per cent say that they are always consulted and the remaining say that they are occasionally consulted. In cultural matters, 50% say that they are not at all consulted. In religious matters a vast majority of 83% say that they are consulted. But among them the majority say that they are consulted sometimes. Only 33% say that they are always consulted.

In decision making, women have poor role. Eighty three per cent say that the role of women in economic as well as educational matters is ineffective and the remaining 17% say partly effective. Even in matters of routine importance also their role is ineffective. However, the position is different in matters concerning religion and marriage. Sixty seven per cent say that they have a role to play in religious matters but partly effective. But their best role is in marriage affairs. While only 17% say that the role is not effective, the rest are happy with their role.

Role of Muslim women in non-formal organizations is also extremely limited. General awareness is poor. Mahila Mandals are almost unknown. There is no effective participation in banking transactions though there is relatively better awareness. They are also generally not bothered because of involvement of men. Public health centres are also generally not known and participation is very almost totally absent. Though there is general awareness about the Mandal Panchayats, there is no effective participation. There are 16 Muslim women members. But their participation is totally ineffective.

Similarly, Muslim women are neither familiar with nor participating in co-operative societies. So far as educational matters are concerned, women have absolutely nothing to do. They have no role to play in village studies, reading rooms and also village festivals.

Whether Muslim women have any role to play in developmental activities? While 50% women say that they have no role, 21% say they play their role and the remaining 29% are neutral. But when asked whether they would like to play their roles, 83% do not want

Awareness of educational programmes is also very poor. Compulsory education is not known to 75%. The remaining have partial knowledge. Integrated Child Development Scheme is known only to 25% and even here they have partial knowledge only. A vast majority are familiar with adult education programme and also family planning. But all these people have only partial knowledge. Vocational education, population education and healh education are known only to a small number.

Some of the social security measures are known to Muslim women. But they have generally partial knowledge. Even though life insurance scheme is there for a long time, only 25% know this and they have only partial knowledge. Health Insurance is known to 8%. Old age pension and widow's pension schemes are known to a vast majorlty. But they have partial knowledge only. Savings schemes like National Savings Certificate and Indira Vikas Patrika are almost unknown.

Awareness of Muslim organizations is also generally very poor. Muslim League is not known to 80%. Baitul-maal is not known to 87%. Though Jamaat-e-Islami and Tableeq-e-Jamaat are working vigorously, awareness among Muslim women is poor. While only 29% women know Jamaat-e-Islami, 40% know Tableeq-e-Jamaat. Mosque committees are known to 43%. However, women say that it is the concern of their men-folk.

Women's organizations are also generally not known. Family planning is familiar. They are not generally opposed to this. But some knowledgeable persons say that the religious prescriptions would not encourage family planning as this would lead to immorality and killing of children.

Twenty five per cent women favour adult education for males and only 25% for adult females. Some women who are in favour of adult education say that the timings, work place, etc. would affect their participation.

Education for children is favoured by a vast majority. Women favour education upto Primary standard for boys and girls (75%). While 75% women favour High School education for boys, only 17% favour for girls. College education is favoured by 42% for the boys and only 8% for girls.

Opinion of Muslim women is clear about employment for women. A vast majority do want to take up some economic activities at home, earn and help the family. They are not keen on being major partners in running the family. They are also not against employment for wages outside the home if the place of work is not far away.

Women are not happy with child labour. They say it is bad. But they would rather like to allow the children go out for work if they do not want to go to schools. Women feel that children would create problems if they neither go to schools nor for work. However, women are not in favour of female children going out for work.

E. Comparative Status

It is generally felt that the Muslims are backward. But the question generally surfaces is how backward are the Muslims in comparison with the Backward Castes and Scheduled Castes. Are they better or equal or worse than either of the other groups ? The situational analysis is briefly summarised and presented here.

There is not much difference between the Muslims and the other groups so far as employment status is concerned. A vast majority of all the groups are employed. Uuemployment is not a problem. But Muslims feel that they are discriminated in public sector for purposes of securing jobs.

A vast majority of all the groups are involved in agricultural sector. However, there are more Muslims (28%) than Scheduled Castes (25%) and more Backward Castes (31%) than Muslims as cultivators. Further, there is a significant change among the Muslim labourers. Because of Land Reforms Act, rural to urban migration and lack of encouragement, the number of Muslim cultivators is dwindling, whereas the situation among the Scheduled Castes and Backward Castes has improved very much. Scheduled Castes who were the tenants and farm labourers of the Muslims are now in better position.

As farm labourers, Muslims are slightly fewer than Backward castes and much fewer than Scheduled Castes. It mean there are more Backward Castes and Scheduled Castes working as farm labourers than Muslims. In this sense, Muslims have a better status. But the present trend is that Muslims, who were once land owners are gradually turning out to be farm labourers, where the Scheduled Castes, the once tenants and labourers, are turning out to be land owners. In the case of the former, it is occupational downward mobility and in the case of the latter, it is just a question of occupational upward mobility. In industrial sector, Muslims are far behind the Backward Castes as well as the Scheduled Castes, both as small industrialists and industrial labourrs.

In Government service too, the Muslims are the worst. While Muslims account for just 6%, the Backward Castes have got into Government service to the extent of 10% and Scheduled Castes 12.5%. Muslims are sore about this. In business, Muslims have the best position. While the Scheduled Castes are not at all involved in business, due to the social stigma attached to them, even the Backward Castes are not in large number. So far as tailoring is concerned, Muslims have the virtual monopoly of it. None of the Backward Castes and Scheduled Castes are involved in this occupation.

The income position gives a different meaning. In the lower income range, Scheduled Castes are more than Muslims and Muslims are more than the Backward Castes (as confined to the respondents). In the middle and higher income range, Muslims are more than either of the groups. In general, Muslims are better than the Backward Castes as well as the Scheduled Castes. But Muslims are still more backward. So far as family income is concerned, Muslims are more than the Scheduled Castes as well as the Backward Castes in the lower income range. There are more Muslims than the Scheduled Castes in the middle income range. However, the Backward Castes are better than the Muslims.

All the three groups are more or less equal so far as land holdings are concerned. They are all marginal farmers. However while Muslims are slightly better placed than Scheduled Castes, there is not much difference between Muslims and Backward Castes. So far as wet lands are concerned, Muslims are slightly better than Backward Castes and much better than Scheduled Castes. However, while Muslims were much better before independence, others are improving their positions now.

Muslims are not the worst lot so far as awareness is concerned. More muslims than either Scheduled Castes are aware of dairy programmes. Muslims have an edge over the other people in matters relating to poultry. Muslims are better than Scheduled Castes, and Backward Castes are better than Muslims so far as awareness of sheep rearing programmes is concerned. Subsidy schemes are known to Muslims as well as Scheduled Castes. Muslims are better than Backward Castes.

So far as awareness of the agricultural programmes is concerned, there is not much difference among all the three groups. A vast majority of all these groups are not aware of the schemes.

However, Muslims are the worst in so far as minor irrigation works are concerned. Scheduled Castes and Backward Castes are better than Muslims so far as social forestry is concerned. Muslims and Backward Castes are equal and Muslims are better than Scheduled Castes so far as sericulture is concerned.

Improved wage scheme is better known to Muslims than Backward Castes, whereas Scheduled Castes are better than Muslims. While 81% Muslims do not know Minimum Wages Act, Backward Castes and Scheduled Castes have better knowledge. All the three groups have poor knowledge so far equal wages for equal work principle is concerned. Scheduled Castes have better awareness of rural employment scheme than Muslims. Muslims and Backward Castes have equally poor knowledge.

Awareness of social legislation is generally very poor among Muslims. Scheduled Castes are better than Muslims in many areas. Even Backward Castes are better than Muslims in many areas like Bonded Labour Legislation. Muslims have very poor knowledge of various health programmes like child care, immunization, dental care, etc. Scheduled Castes and Backward Castes are better than Muslims.

Even in matters relating to social legislation, Muslims are generally far behind the Scheduled Castes and Backward Castes. Animal health scheme is known to more Muslims than either Scheduled Castes or Backward Castes.

While Muslims are sore about the absence of the role of Muslim religious leaders in developmental matters. Scheduled Castes feel that Hindu religious leaders are more harmful.

Eighty three per cent Muslims feel that they are better than Scheduled Castes as well as Backward Castes in general so far as education in concerned.

The majority of the Muslims feel that they are better than

Scheduled Castes as well as Backward Castes. This is more or less the feeling of the Muslims in economic matters too.

In matters of employment, Muslims feel that the Scheduled Castes and Backward Castes are better than Muslims.

CONCLUSIONS

A. Economic Status

1. The study reveals that the economic conditions of rural Muslims in general are not encouraging. The fact that while the heads of the families are mostly involved in cultivation of lands, but the members of the family are working as farm labourers would imply that in course of time, farm labour would be the major occupation of the Muslims.

2. Muslim women are still bound by traditional cultural barriers. They do not like to work on lands of outsiders particularly non-Muslims, as farm labourers unless poverty forces them to yield. Their feeling is that working on the lands of others bring disgrace to the Muslim society.

3. Inspite of lot of importance given for rural industries by the State, involvement of Muslims is extremely negligible. There is no proper motivation besides encouragement to promote cottage industries among them. Traditional occupations like business and tailoring are still favourite professions among Muslims. There is a growing desire for jobs in Government service. But the fact that the representation is very poor would indicate the gap between the desire of the people and the social action of the State. The main grievance of the Muslims that they are neglected in Government as well as public sector stands confirmed by the data presented in the study.

4. The general income position is alarming. The fact that a vast majority of them are still earning not more than Rs. 300 per month would indicate the painful situation of the Muslims. Muslims are in the habit of raising loans from private parties for consumption purposes and this would always pose a danger of remaining in debts and hence development is retarded. But what is more revealing is the fact that even when they desire loans for constructive purposes, they find it very hard to get loans from the public sector. This situation has made them disillusioned and desperate.

5. Muslims who were once land owners and also land lords are in a different situation today. Even though the vast majority of them have lands, the fact that these are all generally small acres of dry land would mean that they are vastly marginal farmers. Another important conclusion that is drawn in the study is that Muslims are in a transition period from landownership to landless farm labourers. The various socio-legal forces like migration and land reforms have altered their socio-economic status. At this rate, in one or two generations all rural Muslims will be landless labourers.

6. The generation gap is on the increase. Their conditions are worsening today than before. Where the general trend among the non-Muslims is upward mobility, among Muslims downward mobility is noticed.

7. Muslims society seems to have no concern about the danger of child-labour. Both boys and girls are involved here. Eventhough they are not involved in health hazardous occupations, increased number of child labourers would not mean better future for the Muslims. Though poverty is the compelling force, very little has been realized that poverty gets increased and perpetuated if the children do not receive better attention, But who

is to guide them ? There is none either among themselves or outsiders.

B. Educational Status

1. Compared to the past, there is a lot of improvement in the literacy status of the Muslims. But still the fact that a little more than 50% are illiterates calls for better efforts to bridge the gap. Higher education beyond upper primary education is neglected.

2. 'Drop-outs' is a great drawback among the Muslims. A vast majority of them drop out either at the lower primary or upper primary level. What is further revealing is the fact that nearly half of the illiterates are reverted illiterates, meaning thereby that these children forget whatever they had learnt in the primary school.

3. The general theory that literacy depends upon the nature of occupation and income is confirmed in the present study. There is better literacy level among cultivators than among farm labourers. Further, literacy status also depends upon the income. Better the income level is, higher is the literacy level.

4. There is a good response from the parents to give education to their children beyond upper primary level. They are also practical in their approach in matters relating to secular education as well as theological education. They do not favour proficiency in theological education as this would not help them earning their bread.

5. The fact that the parents could say what type and what level of education is required for boys and girls and the reasons for which this type of education is required is a positive sign of their mental maturity. It also means that under this encouraging social climate, response of Muslims to educational advancement will be much

more significant if only certain bottlenecks are overcome.

6. Rural educational system is very much handicapped, according to the study. Basic facilities are lacking for long. Inspite of loud announcements made under the Five Year Plans, in practice not much has been done. There is a growing feeling among the Muslims that the Government is least interested in the advancement of the Muslims. At the same time, the study reveals that the teachers and Inspectors of Schools do often have unholy alliances and fail in their duty to help Muslims come up educationally.

7. There is also a deeply rooted thinking among Muslims that higher education should lead to better jobs in the Government. The fact that a few boys had graduated and could not get jobs either worthy of the educational background or at the worst any type of job, makes the parents hesitant to send their children for higher education. This cannot be taken as baseless.

8. Inspite of loud thinking about adult education, it is seen that it has failed by and large. The failure is not so much due to the indifference of the people as is due to the fact that the timings, place, trainor, contents are not relevant. It is strange that preliminary steps to assess the felt needs and cultural conditions of the participants have been neglected.

9. The much publicised propaganda over T.V. about the duty of the parents to have the correct date of birth of their children has very little influence on the people. This is due to various reasons. T.V. is yet to reach areas and therefore its utility is limited. Hardly parents manage to maintain relevant records of the their children.

C. Awareness

1. Awareness which is the basic requirement for participation in developmental activities is very much wanting among the Muslims. The fact that three-fourths of them are totally ignorant and even those who have awareness have only practical awareness would speak volumes of the pathetic situation of the Muslims. Excepting adult education and family planning, none of the other programmes like Integrated Child Development scheme, population education, land improvement scheme, minor irigation programmes, etc. are known to a vast majority. Their ignorance or limited knowledge is a major reason for the relatively poor participation of Muslims rural development.

2. Some of the special measures like the Minority Development Corporation, Minority Commissions are not known to vast majority. This is a very serious issue. What is the use of establishing such organizations when the expected beneficiaries are not familiar with them ?

3. Further, what is still more distressing is the fact that even some of the common socio-religious organizations like Jamaat-e-Islami, Tablique-e-Jamaat and Muslim League are also not widely known among Muslims. Various Boards and Corporations set up by the State for general public, social security measures, Islamic principles of development are also not known to the the majority. It is only in the case of old age and widows pension scheme that the majority are aware. It means that programmes which have been put through with wide publicity and efforts are known to people. It would therefore imply that neither the State or the Muslim leaders have initiated any steps to create awareness and prepare them for participation.

4. Another important conclusion that could be drawn from this study is that Muslim leaders of different categories have neglected the people. Whether they are religious leaders, political leaders or intellectuals, their contribution to the basic requirement of creating awareness is extremely negligible. What is more significant is the fact that the Muslim respondents have no hesitation to acknowledge the services of the Hindu leaders who have done better service to the Muslims.

5. This leads to a very important question. Should there be reservation or special considerations which enable a few individuals come up in life and the developmental benefits are monopolised by them and their families ? Commitment to the development of Muslims would not mean communalism. No Hindu would ever object of the Muslim officers take up the cause of Muslims along with the non-Muslims. On the other hand, if the Muslims are neglected, they tend to remain an eternal burden to the State and Society.

6. Muslim women, as women in general are, desire to work hard and supplement the family income. There are still certain cultural barriers which prevent them from taking jobs outside the family circle. But it is also revealed in the study that when faced with acute poverty, they break the barriers.

7. Another significant conclusion is that women have realised the importance and significance of cottage industries for family income. It is also heartening to note this preparedness for training to improve development skills. This is a positive sign of the rural Muslim women's changing values and attitudes.

8. The study reveals that the rural Muslims have little role to play in family affairs. They hardly participate

and are rarely consulted in many family matters, excepting religious and marriage affairs. It means that the males have virtual domination and women are silent and mute partners of their men-folk.

D. Muslim Women

1. Muslim women are virtually out of social organisations. Their participation even in organizations like Mahila Mandals is almost nil. General awareness of what is going on around the family circle is also extremely poor. Though they are generally aware of mandal panchayats, their participation is ineffective.

2. Neither they are familiar with educational programmes nor are they generally aware of their role in developmental activities. But they are conscious of the importance of family planning. Their awareness of population education, vocational education and health education is very poor.

3. Though several social security measures are in existence for a long time, Muslim women have in general very poor knowledge excepting in the case of old age and widow's pension schemes. Similarly, their awareness of Muslim organizations is also poor. This means not adequate efforts have been put in to create awareness.

4. Educationally women are very backward. Female drop-out is also alarming. Reverted literacy is also a major problem. However, they are in favour of education for children and against child labour.

5. To sum up, Muslim women are generally neglected in all areas of development. They have poor knowledge of the existence and importance of a large number of social, economic and religious organizations of the Muslims. But they are not allergic to participate in

development. Their non-participation is only because of the negative attitude of the males.

E. Comparative Status

1. The question of relative backwardness of Muslims assumes significance in the context of special schemes for the Scheduled Castes and Backward Castes. Answer to this question is a bit difficult because of lack of emperical studies. However, a few broad conclusions can be drawn based on the present study.

2. There is a strong feeling among Muslims that they are discriminated in so far as jobs in Government and Public sectors are concerned. They feel that they are far behind the Scheduled Castes and Backward Castes. Downward mobility is one of the chief characteristics of the Muslim situation.

3. For various reasons such as Land Reforms Act, Rural-urban migration and lack of input for development, more and more Muslims are losing lands and the present condition is that Muslims are slightly better than Scheduled Castes, but Backward Castes are slightly better than Muslims. Scheduled Castes who were tenants and farm labourers of the Muslims are advancing better than Muslims. In industrial sector too Muslims are far behind the Scheduled Castes and Backward Castes.

4. Muslims have still retained their virtual monopoly of tailoring profession and the Scheduled Castes as well as the Backward Castes are nowhere. Business is still a favourable occupation of the Muslims as against the Backward Castes and Scheduled Castes.

5. The income position of the Muslims in general is better than the Scheduled Castes as well as the Backward Castes.

6. While the Backward Castes and Scheduled Castes are getting more and more organized to fight for their rights, Muslims are getting divided and disillusioned. Factionalism and disharmony over petty considerations have degenerated Muslims. The general feeling that Muslims are a well knit social group is a myth. The entire development work gets stalled because of the petty, selfish and narrow outlook among the Muslims.
7. Muslim religious leaders have not yet realised that they can play a vital role in ensuring positive changes and assured progress if only they appeal to the Muslim masses to follow Islamic blue-print for development. Political leadership of the Muslims is generally a great failure. Muslim masses are dis-illusioned with their selfish political leaders. On the other hand, Muslims repose better faith in the Hindu leadership. Intellectuals and elite have hardly made any contribution to their development. Muslim officers too have generally let the Muslim masses down. Their indifference, hesitation, apathy and evasiveness would expose them in general and a fresh approach is needed. Why should there be reservation or agitation for more and more representation to the Muslims at higher levels in State administration if these officers cannot discharge their legitimate and reasonable duties ? This is the feeling of the educated rural Muslim youths.
8. Muslim socio-religious organizations have virtually failed in initiating programmes for Muslim cause. The fact that general awareness of the very existence of the various programmes is lacking among Muslim masses would definitely speak against these organization. Preaching Islamic ways of life, if properly done, could also kindle interest among Muslims to take advantage of the State policies and programmes. Organizations of the Scheduled castes and Backward Castes are doing better service to these people.

9. What is further distressing is that in general the numerical dominant position of the Muslims has turned out to be a disadvantageous and harmful factor rather than a supporting force. Internal feuds over small considerations have led to inaction. The real spirit of Islam for development and progress through unity and understanding is painfully missing. But the position is better among the Scheduled castes who are inspired by the teachings of Dr. Ambedkar.

10. On the other hand, the positive thinking of many Hindu leaders in non-Muslim dominant villages has been a helping factor. Muslims in general, are better placed in non-Muslim dominant areas. They have better awareness and understanding and also better participation in these non-Muslim dominant villages.

11. The study also reveals that in general Muslims are losing their traditional superior status when compared to the Scheduled caste and Backward Castes. In quite a few areas, Scheduled Castes and Backward Castes have already overtaken the Muslims and in some areas it may take some more time. This is due to two factors. First, the Muslims themselves need to be blamed. Their apathy for development goes against them. Secondly, the State has generally neglected the Muslim cause. It is true that the 20 Point Economic Programmes and 15 Point Programmes mean a lot for Muslim development. But the present study makes it clear beyond shadow of doubt that these are all paper-tigers and election stunts.

12. It may be true that the intention of the political parties and the apex body of the administration is positive and helpful to the Muslim cause. But the indifferent role of the bureaucracy and the failure of the apex body to

monitor and evaluate implementation of t e programmes would kill the policies and prescriptions.

13. The Scheduled Castes in particular are in a better position to get their share. Non-implementation becomes a major issue for discussion in the State legislatures and the Parliament. But who bothers about the failure of the administrative machinery so far as Muslims are concerned ? This is the message that the present study gives.

F. Regional Differences

1. One of the main objectives of the study is to examine the gaps, if any, between the Old Mysore region and North Karnataka region. This is very important from the angle of removing major imbalances and ensure development with distributive justice.

2. The study reveals very significantly that in general Old Mysore region is far ahead of North Karnataka region in many areas of development. Educationally and economically, Mysore region has achieved better progress. There is a greater awareness among Muslims of Old Mysore region.

3. This means that our planners have not paid adequate attention to the regional imbalances. The findings of the study also confirm the stand taken by the Government of Karnataka that these two regions have major areas of differences and therefore the Hyderabad Karnataka Development Board has been set up for identifying the areas of differences and appropriate action for narrowing down the gap.

RECOMMENDATIONS

Since the study is utilitarian in its nature, a few major recommendations become inevitable. These recommendations are likely to help the policy makers, administrators, Muslim leaders and the Muslims masses themselves.

A. Role of the State

1. Separate Plan

The State has to evolve a separate plan for a particular and definite period for the development of Minorities in general and Muslims in particular. A specific outlay has to be earmarked. In other words, the policies and prescriptions enunciated for the benefit of the Scheduled Castes will have to be followed. A special component plan as in the case of the Scheduled Castes is essential.

A fully qualified and competent representative of the Muslims should invariably be included on the State Planning Board. Similarly, due representation should be given to Muslims at all levels and on all committees designated for rural development in particular.

Specific programmes should be formulated for Muslim women and child development. Mahila Mandals and Integrated Child Development Schemes be encouraged so as to include Muslims too. Since Muslim children are virtually neglected both by the State and the Society and children are great asset for National development, potential resources should be fully and truely identified, harnessed and utilised.

2. Awareness Creation

Awareness creation is the need of the hour. All policies and programmes of the State should be brought to the notice of the people through wide publicity. Radio, T.V., Newspaper, village meetings, Mandal Panchayats, should be some of the means. Village school teachers should also be involved. Village level functionaries of the Government should take necessary steps to educate the people.

3. Land Grant Policy

The various land grant and land utilization policies of the State should also include the Muslims as done in the case of the Scheduled Castes. Necessary inputs and loans be made easily available to the Muslim farmers.

4. Small Scale Industries and Animal Husbandry

Since Muslim women in particular have expressed their willingness to get involved in small scale cottage industries, fresh efforts should be made by all concerned including Khadi and Village Industries Board to identify the needs and resources and ensure relevant help.

Animal husbandry schemes be made available to them. Women in particular can take advantage of the dairy and poultry schemes.

5. Minority Development Corporation

The Minority Development Corporation should not be ornamental and politically motivated. Its structure and functions need to be radically altered so as to enable the Corporation study the need of the poor minorities and initiate measures. The Corporation should be a permanent structure and delinkeed from political patronage. It should consist of social scientists, social workers and committed elite.

The grants and loans from the State should be quite reasonable to enable the Corporation discharge its functions. It should be entrusted with the task of improving socio-economic conditions of the minorities. Implementation of the 20 Point Programmes and 15 Points Programmes should be entrusted to the Corporation.

The Corporation should take up periodical surveys to assess the situation. It should have links with voluntary organizations, state departments and other relevant institutions. Its report shall be placed before the State legislature for necessary action.

6. Minority Commission

Similary, the Minority Commission should be made to function effectively and be a permanent body. It should have legal status and have powers under the Commission of Enquiry Act. It should consist of eminent persons representing different shades or groups. Social scientist, social workers, lawyers, retired judges and bureaucrats, educationists, economists, doctors, engineers and so on be on the Commission. It should not have political affiliations and biases.

The Minority Commission should be a monitoring and evaluation body and as such should be linked with Minority Development Corporation so far as socio-economic programmes are concerned. Minority Development Corporation would therefore be an executive body and as such be accountable to the Minority Commission.

Minority Commission should also be in charge of National Emotional Integration programmes, communal riot situations and so on. It should have powers to probe into the functioning of the administrative machinary and injustices and discrimination practised against the Minorities.

Further, there should be linkage between State Minority Commission and National Minority Commission. The latter should have powers to guide and assist the former wherever needed. Since the State policies and Central policies may differ, it is better to have working relationship between the two Commissions.

7. Reservation Policy

The reservation policy of the State should undergo significant changes. Quota system to ensure proportionate representation in all areas and at all levels is the only solution to the problems of the minorities. Whether it is in Government or public sector or even in private sectors, there should be adequate representation to the minorities. Default should be seriously viewed and punitive action be taken.

Even in educational and economic development programmes, State has to ensure proportionate representation. It should mean justice to them, and not pampering or appeasement. As Dr. B.R. Ambedkar has rightly pointed out, "the concept of Minority is a reality in democracy and any special measure is a just need and not a greed."

8. Skill Development

Skill development work is virtually alien to Muslims, though often they are capable of making advances. Therefore, State should contemplate schemes for developing and improving the skills of Muslims in general and women in particular.

Since women find it difficult to go to towns and cities to receive training, it would be desirable to start training centres in the concerned villages or in the centre of a cluster of villages. Of course, these schemes could be for women of different social groups.

9. Adult Education

Adult education system should be restructured. It is just not a question of teaching alphabets. But it is a question of preparing them to participate in development activities. Women have to be roped in. Course contents should be restructured to attract Muslim women. Perhaps a little religious touch might be useful. Teachers should be females and classes should be held exclusively for women and in their own areas, to the extent possible.

Non-formal education should include health education, population education, awareness of the State policies and programmes, nutrition education, parents responsibilities towards their children and so on.

10. Urdu Schools

The standard of Urdu Primary schools should be improved. The Heads of schools and the Inspectors should be held responsible and accountable for better social behaviour. Adequate buildings with necessary infra-structural facilities must be provided.

There seems to be an imperative need to experiment with the concept of Integrated Schools where Urdu and Kannada medium schools co-exist in the same compound and parts of the buildings. But the management will be common. That is, on rotation basis, Head Master of one linguistic school should be appointed as Head Master of both the linguistic schools or Urdu school Head Master should look after Kannada medium school and vice-versa.

The advantages of such a type of school is that there would be better social control over the teachers, would promote the concept of emotional integration among the teachers and students. When children of different social groups mix together and play together, a better social climate will be produced.

11. Muslim Women's Organizations

Both the State and the Muslim society should encourage Mahila Mandals either exclusively or in collaboration with the non-Muslim women. It is not that Muslim women cannot be motivated at all. Efforts made by a few voluntary organizations have proved that Muslim women could be pursuaded to form their Organizations. Of course, there will be initial problems, mostly due to cultural barriers. But when once there is 'take-off', further progress is assured.

12. Youths and Drop-outs

Muslims youths are at cross-road. They do not have enough work. They do not have any one to guide. Therefore, they become often a nuisance. Youths should be motivated to participate in development work. Youth clubs, though not exclusively for Muslims, should be encouraged by the State to get involved in development works. Youth training centres should be organized for clusters of villages. Mobile units of trainers would be adequate.

Children who drop-out at early age get involved in all sorts of work. Though sometimes they are involved in productive works, they need proper guidance and orientation. In order to provide a healthy environment to them, it would be desirable to organize children's clubs and allow the children themselves to manage the show under the guidance of the social workers. Children's clubs can take up matters relating to values, skills, general knowledge, sharing of experiences, health and nutrition issues, formulation of projects for proper utilization of their resources. School dropouts can be provided with non formal education so that they remain literates and knowledgeable.

13. Girl-Child

Girl child is generally neglected. She suffers from various handicaps. Parents should be made aware of their duties. Campaigns should be arranged to create awareness of children's rights in general and girl child in particular.

14. Role of Bureaucrats

Officers in charge of rural development should play their role effectively and faithfully irrespective of religious background. Muslim officers should be held responsible and be punishable if they neglect the Muslims whatever be the circumstances. The policies and the programmes must be effectively implemented. Annual reports should be called for and their performance should be evaluated.

It is also true that even the non-Muslim officers should play helpful role. Discrimination against the Minorities should be viewed as an offence and punishment be inflicted. In other words, whether the officers are Muslims or non-Muslims, what is required is that the Officers should be fair, impartial and helpful to the people of all groups.

15. Religious Leaders

Religious leaders should play a dynamic and constructive role to motivate Muslims to be hard working, responsible and to participate in development works. Islamic blue-print for development of Muslims should be focussed. Since Islamic principles are realistic and humane, it is easier to rope in Muslim youths, in particular, in development works. Later on, these leaders could also play much better role as done by the Christian Priests.

Congregation prayers on Fridays, could also be made use of. Muslim Organizations like Jamaat-e-Islami and Tagliq-e-Jamaat should play a better role by taking up socio-economic programmes. Government should encourage them within reasonable limits.

16. Muslim Solidarity

Though outwardly Muslims give the impression that they are a united and strong force, in reality they are not so. Faction ridden Muslim society needs a dynamic leadership. They should be motivated to mobilize all their resources for development. They should be encouraged to develop the spirit of futurity. They should be prepared to face challenges and take advantage of the development tempo.

17. Voluntary Organizations

For all this, voluntary organizations consisting of selfless and committed youths are inevitable. Both the State and the Muslim society should encourage and patronize such voluntary organizations. These organizations should change the attitudes and approach of Muslims towards development.

These voluntary organizations should be encouraged to set up Pre-Primary schools and motivate parents to send their children to primary schools regularly and purposefully. Similarly, school drop-outs should be motivated to learn out-of-school and improve their behaviour and skills.

18. Wakf Board

Wakf Board and Wakf Development Corporation should play a vital role in Muslim development. The vast resources of the Wakf Board should be properly identified and taken over by the Board for proper utilization. The Board and the Corporation should have fully competent members who have vision, commitment and selflessness to take up the cause of Muslim development.

19. Regional Planning

Another important recommendation is the need to correct regional imbalances. The State has to use its planning machinary to find out regional disparities of much significance and then adopt appropriate schemes. While Old Mysore region in general is relatively more progressive than the North Karnataka region, there are still internal differences within. In Old Mysore area some of the maidan areas are more progressive than the malnad region.

Similarly, within the North Karnataka region, Bombay-Karnataka area is more progressive than the Hyderabad-Karnatak area. Therefore, regional planning is inevitable while tackling the development problems of the Muslims in rural Karnataka.

Index